DOG OF DISCOVERY

for Patrick —
a life of adventure,
discovery, and love!
Laurence
Pringle
2010

DOG OF DISCOVERY

A Newfoundland's Adventures with Lewis and Clark

by
Laurence Pringle

CALKINS CREEK
AN IMPRINT OF HIGHLIGHTS
Honesdale, Pennsylvania

To Sarah Dorothy Biggs
—may your journey into the uncharted territory
of life be full of adventure, discovery,
and love

Credits: title page, pp. 13, 24, 33, 42, 58, 65, 73, 93, 101, 126, 132, 140, drawings by Meryl Henderson; endpaper and p. 15 maps, Tim Gillner; p. 9, Independence National Historical Park; pp. 14, 43, 59, *Animals, 1419 Copyright-Free Illustrations of Mammals, Birds, Fish, Insects, etc.*, Dover Publications; p. 18, photo of a reproduction of rifle carried by the men of the Lewis and Clark Expedition courtesy of Village Restoration and Consulting, Claysburg, PA; p. 21, Yale Collection of Western Americana, Beinecke Rare Book and Manuscript Library; p. 26 (detail), E.S. Paxson, Montana Historical Society; p. 32, Wayne Arnst; pp. 36, 89, American Philosophical Society; p.38 Interior—Sports Fisheries & Wildlife; p. 41, Ann & Rob Simpson; p. 46, Oregon Historical Society, negative numbers OR HI 38090 and OR HI 38091; p. 51, Joslyn Art Museum, Omaha, NE; p.57, Kit Wray, from "Finding Sacagawea," *Highlights for Children*, November 1999, © 1999 by Highlights for Children, Inc., Columbus, OH; p. 82, nutcracker, Emma Ahart, woodpecker, Bill Proud; p. 122, Montana Historical Society, Helena; p. 133, National Archives, Maps and Plans Group, Special Media Archives Division, College Park, MD; p. 135, United States Mint. Journal quotations reprinted from the University of Nebraska Press edition of *The Journals of Lewis and Clark*, edited by Gary E. Moulton.

Calkins Creek
An Imprint of Highlights
815 Church Street
Honesdale, Pennsylvania 18431
Printed in the United States of America

The Library of Congress has cataloged the hardcover edition of this book as follows:

Library of Congress Cataloging-in-Publication Data

Pringle, Laurence.
Dog of discovery / by Laurence Pringle ; illustrated by Meryl Henderson. — 1st ed.
[152] p. : col. ill. ; cm.
Includes bibliographical references and index.
Summary: A detailed account of the Lewis and Clark expedition features the dog
that was its most unusual member. Selections from the actual journals of
Lewis and Clark appear throughout the text.
ISBN: 978-1-59078-028-2 (hc) • ISBN: 978-1-59078-267-5 (pb)
1. Lewis and Clark Expedition (1803–1806)—Juvenile nonfiction. 2. Explorers—Nonfiction—
Juvenile literature. [1. Lewis and Clark Expedition (1803–1806)—Nonfiction.
2. Dogs—Nonfiction. 3. West (U.S.)—Discovery and exploration—Nonfiction.
4. Explorers—Nonfiction—Juvenile literature.] I. Henderson, Meryl. II. Title.
[F] 21 CIP 2002
2002102046

First edition
First Boyds Mills Press paperback edition, 2004
The text of this book is set in Minion.
The sidebar text is Minion Italic.

20 19 18 17 16 15 14 13 12 11 10 9

Acknowledgments

———⊷•⊶———

The author is especially grateful to Jay Rasmussen for fact-checking both the manuscript and illustrations. Mr. Rasmussen, president of the Oregon chapter of the Lewis and Clark Trail Heritage Foundation, helped the artists avoid repetition of errors that are so widespread in illustrations of the expedition. He applied his deep knowledge of the Lewis and Clark expedition to the text and to every quotation from the journals, and pointed out the instances where the author used conjecture.

The author also thanks Judi Adler of Sweetbay Newfoundlands, Alex Kealy of Fetch, and Richard and Flo Symington for their knowledge of the Newfoundland breed; author Gail Karwoski for her generous help throughout the project; jacket artist Patrick O'Brien and interior artist Meryl Henderson for their accurate and appealing illustrations; editor Carolyn Yoder and copy editor Susan McClosky for their keen-eyed yet light-handed work on the text; and production manager Alice Cummiskey, designer Tim Gillner, Jo Ann Lloyd, and other staff members of Boyds Mills Press for their swift but able work on this book.

Contents

Introduction
Dog of Discovery

Meriwether Lewis

William Clark

IN 1803 A SMALL GROUP OF MEN SET OUT on one of the most extraordinary journeys in American history. Led by Meriwether Lewis and William Clark, their goal was to explore unmapped territory west of the young United States, all the way to the Pacific Ocean.

This expedition, called the Corps of Discovery, faced many known and unknown dangers. Despite great hardship and many dangerous encounters with rattlesnakes, grizzly bears, and wild river rapids, the Corps of Discovery traveled more than eight thousand miles and returned triumphantly in the summer of 1806. Thanks to the richly detailed journals of Lewis, Clark, and others, today we can relive the day-to-day adventures of the Corps of Discovery—and of its most unusual member, Seaman, a Newfoundland dog.

This giant dog was no mere pet. Meriwether Lewis had picked the perfect breed for great adventures on wilderness rivers and rugged mountains. As a hunter, retriever, and guard dog, Seaman was a valuable member of the expedition. As Meriwether Lewis's companion, he was present at many key events. Like all members of the Corps of Discovery, Seaman suffered from hunger, insect bites, and injuries. He risked his life many times.

With his keen senses of smell and hearing, Seaman experienced the Lewis and Clark expedition as only a dog could. Alas, he kept no journal, but his story also is a basic part of a remarkable expedition. In this book, Seaman serves as an unusual focus as the events of the expedition unfold.

Although Lewis and Clark have been called "the writingest explorers of all time," historians and others wish they had given more details about some subjects, such as the Shoshone teenager Sacagawea and her baby and Lewis's dog. Seaman is mentioned on different dates by Lewis, Clark, or Sergeant John Ordway. Many of these journal entries report the same incident; they are listed on pages 141–142. There is one eight-month period—from August 17, 1805, until April 11, 1806—during which Seaman is not mentioned at all.

In *Dog of Discovery* I have included every incident involving Seaman from the journals and also added "informed guesses" (conjecture) about Seaman's actions. We know Seaman was a dog, so of course he scratched at fleas and used his extraordinary sense of smell to learn about his surroundings. We know he was a Newfoundland. Knowledge of that breed tells us that Seaman was good with children; enjoyed cold, snowy weather; and loved being in water. However, the journals do not once mention Seaman wagging his tail, or tell exactly how Lewis stopped the blood spurting from his dog's artery. Thus, in this carefully researched account of the Lewis and Clark expedition, I have added several dozen actions taken by Seaman, or by people in relation to him, that in all likelihood occurred but are not part of the historical record.

Finally, there is the matter of Seaman's fate. For many years there was speculation that he may not have survived the journey home. Seaman's name does not appear in the journals describing the last two months of travel down the Missouri. In the year 2000, however, new evidence was reported that he had indeed returned home with his master, Meriwether Lewis, so I have made further assumptions about Seaman's actions in the summer of 1806.

With or without the "informed guesses" I have added, there is no doubt that Seaman was a brave, loyal dog and an important member of the Corps of Discovery.

Chapter

I

A Journey
into the Unknown

THE NEWBORN PUPS WERE COVERED with shiny black fur, but their eyes had not yet opened. Their Newfoundland mother licked them clean and guided them to their first meal of milk. As they nursed, the pups made squeaky little grunts. At this stage they all looked pretty much alike, and, of course, no one could imagine that one of the male pups would someday be a national hero.

The pups were probably born in Pittsburgh, Pennsylvania, perhaps near the busy waterfront on the Ohio River. The year was probably 1802. As the pups grew up to be frisky young dogs, the fate of that one male Newfoundland was being decided, unwittingly, by Thomas Jefferson, the third president of the United States.

Thomas Jefferson
Third U.S. President,
1801–1809

Thomas Jefferson was a brilliant man—a lawyer, a scientist, an inventor, an architect, and a philosopher. He was also an extraordinary president. In the early 1800s it seemed inevitable to many that North America would eventually be, like Europe, divided into numerous small countries. Jefferson envisioned an "Empire of Liberty" stretching from coast to coast and took bold steps to make that a reality.

Long before he became president, Jefferson dreamed that the young nation would someday stretch from the Atlantic to the Pacific. When he took office in the spring of 1801, the Mississippi River marked the western border of the United States.

Beyond the Mississippi lay a vast land called the Louisiana Territory that was claimed by France and Spain. And beyond the Rocky Mountains, which marked the western boundary of Louisiana, lay more little-known territory that stretched to the Pacific Ocean. Much of it was claimed by Spain, with a northern part—the Oregon Territory— claimed by Spain, Russia, Great Britain, and the United States. The United States' claim was based partly on the explorations of Captain Robert Gray, who in 1792 sailed partway up a river that flowed into the Pacific. He named the river after his ship, the *Columbia Rediva*.

Using information from Captain Gray and others who

sailed trading ships, mapmakers drew some details of the Pacific Northwest coastline. However, between the Pacific and the Mississippi River lay a vast landscape full of mystery. Thomas Jefferson was hungry for knowledge about this unknown two-thirds of North America. He read every available scrap of information about western North America, including reports of traders who ventured west to buy furs from the Indians.

What treasures and dangers lay beyond the western horizon? Some scientists believed that explorers might find woolly mammoths and giant sloths roaming there. Jefferson was told of a huge mountain of pure salt somewhere on the Great Plains. Most intriguing of all were reports that led Jefferson to believe that a mountain range—called Rocky or Stony—might be no taller than the Appalachians and could easily be crossed. If this was true, people and trade goods could travel by boat up the Missouri River, go easily over-land at the Continental Divide, then float down the Columbia or another river to the Pacific.

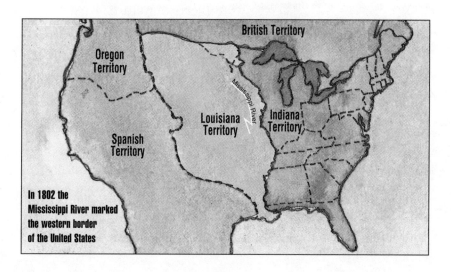

In 1802 the Mississippi River marked the western border of the United States

The first step toward finding this route, and toward somehow making the West part of the United States, was to send out an exploratory expedition. By 1802 Jefferson knew just the right man to lead such an expedition: Meriwether Lewis.

A fellow Virginian and an army officer, Lewis had proved to be an able leader at frontier outposts. In 1801, soon after Jefferson became president, he wrote to Lewis, asking him to be his personal secretary and aide. Lewis agreed. Meriwether Lewis hadn't had much schooling, but he learned quickly as the president taught him many skills that would be valuable on an expedition, such as collecting and identifying plants, using navigation instruments, and writing. In February 1803 the president wrote, "Capt. Lewis is brave, prudent, habituated to the woods, & familiar with Indian manners & character. He is not regularly educated, but he possesses a great mass of accurate information on all the subjects of nature."

President Jefferson asked Lewis to lead the expedition.

In these days of swift communication and travel, life in the early 1800s seems amazingly slow. People and mail and other goods traveled at the pace of horses and boats. Jefferson's letter to Lewis of February 23, 1801, took eleven days to travel from Washington, D.C., to Pittsburgh. Lewis set out almost immediately for Washington, but rain, poor roads, and a lame horse made his trip a twenty-two-day journey.

Congress would have to allot money for the trip, so Lewis estimated the cost of such a mission. He kept it as low as possible. For an expedition involving no more than a dozen men, one officer, and some boats, he judged the cost to be $2,500. Congress approved this amount.

In the first half of 1803 Lewis prepared for this great journey into the unknown. He learned more about using instruments to record the expedition's route, about plant and animal identification, about first aid and medicine. Meanwhile, the president prepared a list of goals for the Corps of Discovery.

Jefferson conferred with scientists and with other advisors. Since Congress had authorized this venture, some of the expedition's goals were to learn about the agricultural and trading possibilities in the West. Not until June 20, 1803, did the president give Meriwether Lewis an official list of instructions. The list was long, diverse, challenging. Foremost was to explore the Missouri River and find "the most direct & practicable water communication across this continent." Part of this challenge involved making good maps of a vast new territory.

The president instructed Lewis to learn as much as possible about Native Americans—their names, populations, languages, customs. Lewis was to try to establish friendly relations with the Indian tribes he met and to encourage trade with the United States.

Jefferson was also curious about soils, minerals, fossils, plants, animals, and climate. Lewis was told that all discoveries and observations were "to be taken with great pains & accuracy, to be entered distinctly and intelligibly" in journals.

➤ March, 1803

Long before these official goals were issued, the president and Meriwether Lewis planned the expedition and discussed the supplies that would be needed, from cooking kettles to books that would help identify plants and minerals. Imagine trying to figure out the needs for such a journey of uncertain distance and indefinite time!

In March, Lewis visited the U.S. Army arsenal in Harpers Ferry, Virginia, and ordered fifteen of the finest rifles made.

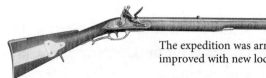

The expedition was armed with Pennsylvania long rifles, improved with new locks at the Harpers Ferry arsenal.

Lewis also bought flints and steels that could be used for starting fires. (Matches that are so common today did not exist.) Flint is a hard quartz stone that gives off sparks when struck with steel. Campfires could be started by striking sparks into dry tinder material, perhaps with some gunpowder added. Sparks from flints also ignited the gunpowder in the rifles.

Later, in Pennsylvania, he ordered fifteen more as well as 200 pounds of gunpowder and 400 pounds of lead. Rifles, lead, and gunpowder would be vital, both for defense and for killing animals for food. The expedition could carry flour, sugar, and salt but would need to live off the land as much as possible.

≫ April, 1803

In Philadelphia, Meriwether Lewis bought many nonperishable items. The most costly purchase, for $250, was a chronometer, an exceptionally precise timepiece needed to find the longitude of a place for mapmaking purposes.

In Philadelphia Lewis also bought a four-volume dictionary that was on the entire journey. This "Dictionary of Arts and Science" contained medical information and was more like an encyclopedia than a dictionary. It was certainly not used to check spelling. Neither Lewis nor Clark had had much formal education. Like most Americans of those times, they used creative spelling and punctuation in their journals, as shown in the quotations used in this book. Their spelling led to puzzlement and controversy about some events and places described in the journals.

Lewis's shopping list included axes, fishhooks, candles, mosquito netting, dried soup, and such items as scissors, small mirrors, beads, thimbles, knives, and combs that could be used mostly for trading with the Indians or as presents for them. He also bought ink powder and paper. The ink powder would be mixed

18

with water in a small container called an inkstand whenever Lewis and others wrote in their journals.

⇒ June 19, 1803

Meriwether Lewis realized that the expedition would need more than a dozen men, and more than one officer. Jefferson agreed and also approved Lewis's request to invite William Clark to join the expedition as co-captain. Lewis and Clark had become friends while serving in the army. Clark was a fine leader of men and had more experience than Lewis in dealing with Indians and in exploring by boat and canoe.

In his letter to Clark, Lewis described the plan and its preparation. He offered Clark the chance to be co-captain of the expedition. He concluded, "If therefore there is anything . . . in this enterprise, which would induce you to participate with me in it's fatiegues, it's dangers and it's honors, believe me there is no man on earth with whom I should feel equal pleasure in sharing them as with yourself."

Lewis's letter from Washington took nearly a month to reach Clark in Kentucky. Clark wrote two letters sent about a week apart. Both reached Lewis on August 3. Clark's response to Lewis:

"My friend I join you with hand & Heart."

⇒ July 4, 1803

While Lewis waited for Clark's reply, President Jefferson released extraordinary news that had arrived by ship from Paris. The United States had been trying to purchase New Orleans and its surrounding area from the French. Instead,

France sold the entire Louisiana Territory to the United States for $15 million. This more than doubled the size of the nation on its twenty-seventh birthday. It also made the Lewis and Clark expedition all the more important. Instead of a secretive venture into foreign territory, it had become an exploration of a huge new part of the United States.

July–August, 1803

Lewis and Clark were to meet in September. In the meantime they took steps to find the kind of men they wanted on the expedition: young, mostly unmarried frontiersmen, especially those with experience as hunters and boatmen or with other skills, such as carpentry.

The rifles, trade goods, and other supplies were being carried by wagon from Philadelphia to Pittsburgh, where the expedition would begin by heading down the Ohio River. Meriwether Lewis traveled to Pittsburgh to check on the construction of a fifty-five-foot-long keelboat that would carry most of the expedition's cargo. The men would also use one or more smaller flat-bottomed boats called pirogues.

The keelboat was supposed to be completed by July 20 but the shipbuilder fell behind schedule. It was promised for July 31, then August 13 but was still not ready.

Each day Lewis visited the boatbuilder's shop, "alternately persuading and threatening." He was frustrated. A drought

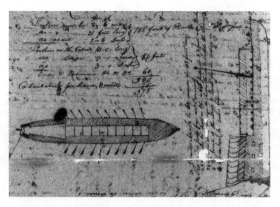

In his journal entry of January 21, 1804, William Clark drew these two views of the keelboat that had been built in Pittsburgh. The boat measured fifty-five feet long and eight feet wide. It was a sturdy craft—able to carry twelve tons of supplies—but hard to manage in the mighty Missouri River. Its sail helped at times, but most of the heavy boat's upriver progress was the result of men using oars, poles, or tow ropes.

Clark drew a side view and an overhead view of the keelboat.

caused the water level of the Ohio River to drop lower and lower, exposing sandbars and other obstacles to boats. This would make travel more difficult, and the expedition that had been so carefully planned was already behind schedule.

❧ August, 1803

Out of this troubling delay in Pittsburgh came one good thing: Meriwether Lewis bought a young Newfoundland dog. Lewis must have valued the dog highly since he paid $20 for it. In those times a man would happily accept the same amount for a month's hard work.

The Newfoundland breed has never been common in the United States and was certainly rare in early-nineteenth-century Pittsburgh.

No one knows whether Lewis bought the dog on impulse or had long hoped to have a Newfoundland. Some people believe that this breed originated in Scandinavia or in northern Spain, but its true origins are unknown. These dogs are famous for rescuing people from water. In 1919 a gold medal was awarded to a Newfoundland that helped save twenty shipwrecked people.

However, Newfoundlands were renowned for their swimming ability, for rescuing people, and for retrieving animals and objects from the water. They were also valued as gentle, loyal companions to ships' captains. They were often called ship dogs or sea dogs. Meriwether Lewis called his dog Seaman.

❧ August 31, 1803

The keelboat was finally finished early in the morning and was loaded and underway by 11 A.M. Seaman explored the boat, sniffing all sorts of bundles that were stored on deck and also taking in the scent of the crewmen. Most of them were hired temporarily. Others would take over when Lewis reached William Clark far down the Ohio River.

On this day Meriwether Lewis wrote the first entry in his journal of the expedition. On the first page of a small leather-bound notebook, he reported slow progress. Even though they were aided by the downstream current, the river was so low that the men had to get out and pull or lift the boat through shallow areas.

For almost two centuries, scholars and others writing about the Lewis and Clark expedition called the dog Scannon. However, the handwriting in the journals was often hard to read. In 1985 historian Donald Jackson carefully examined every mention of the dog in the original journals and discovered the true name: Seaman. Jackson's finding was supported in February 2000, when historian James Holmberg reported Seaman's name inscribed on a dog collar that existed in 1814.

"much fatiegued after labouring with my men all day . . . gave my men some whiskey and retired to rest at 8 OClock."

❧ September 11, 1803

Underway each day about sunrise, Lewis and his crew

struggled down the Ohio. Sometimes they made good progress by steady rowing or even by hoisting the keelboat's square sail. More often they had to get into the water several times a day to free the boat.

On this day the keelboat moved easily down a straight section of the Ohio. Riding in the bow, Seaman began to bark at something he saw in the water. Gray squirrels were crossing the river, swimming from the western to the eastern shore. Lewis yelled, commanding the dog to get a squirrel.

Seaman did not hesitate. He leaped into the river and swam toward a squirrel with powerful strokes. Catching it, he quickly turned and swam back to the boat. Lewis sent Seaman out again and again. That night, after twenty-six miles of travel, the crew had squirrel for dinner. "they wer fat and I thought them when fryed a pleasent food," Lewis wrote.

There have been several reports of mass movements of tree squirrels, usually gray squirrels, in the eastern half of the United States. They occur when squirrel populations are high and may help reduce overcrowding and competition for food. Squirrels often drown while trying to cross rivers and lakes.

⇒ September 12, 1803

"we were obliged to cut a channel through the gravel with our spade and canoe paddles and then drag the boat through we were detained about 4 hours before we accomplished this task." While the crew labored, Seaman frolicked in the shallows and swam around the keelboat. The feet of Newfoundlands are partly webbed, their legs straight and strongly muscled. The men continued to be impressed with Seaman's swimming ability.

❧ September 15, 1803

The unusual squirrel migration continued—"caught by means of my dog several squirrels, attempting to swim the river," wrote Lewis. Seaman earned words of praise and friendly pats on the head from the crew. Though he often napped while the men pulled on their oars, Seaman was already showing his prowess as a hunter and retriever. He was becoming a valuable member of the crew.

❧ Early October, 1803

The keelboat floated through a wild countryside dotted with small settlements. As the Ohio River broadened and deepened, the pace downstream quickened. While pausing for a few days in Cincinnati, Lewis wrote to President Jefferson. When his letter reached the president in late October, Jefferson learned about the delays that would keep the expedition from advancing up the Missouri River before winter. Lewis aimed to spend the winter beside the Mississippi River near St. Louis.

❧ October 14, 1803

The keelboat tied up on the north shore of the Ohio, at the town of Clarksville in the Indiana Territory. With his big black dog trotting alongside, Lewis quickly set out for the home of William Clark.

Not having met face-to-face for several years, the two men shook hands heartily. Almost instantly they began talking about the expedition. Seaman sensed the excitement in Lewis's voice. He barked and pranced around the men, wagging his tail.

Clark asked about the huge dog. As he fondled Seaman's ears and buried his fingers in the dog's thick coat, Seaman inhaled the scents from William Clark's hands and clothes. Clark's unique scent was stored deep in the dog's memory.

Seaman soon met another man—tall and dark-skinned—who would prove to be a valuable member of the expedition. Simply called York, he was William Clark's slave.

❧ November 11, 1803

In the following weeks, Seaman learned the scents of more than twenty men who eagerly joined the expedition. One,

About Clark's age, York had been given to him at an early age. They grew up together as master and slave. Many years would pass before slavery was outlawed in the United States as a result of the Civil War, 1861–1865.

hired on this date, was George Drouillard. He had exactly the skills that were vital to the success of the expedition. He was an excellent hunter and scout with knowledge of Indian languages and of sign language, which could be used when all other languages failed. In their journals, both Lewis and Clark misspelled Drouillard's name, usually as "Drewyer" (which is how this French name is pronounced).

❧ November 14, 1803

At the end of the day the keelboat and pirogues reached the mouth of the Ohio River. The expedition paused for a few days before heading up the mighty Mississippi. Each clear night Lewis taught Clark what he had learned about using a sextant and the movement of stars to record the exact location of the expedition. And as they traveled, Clark shared his expertise at estimating the distance traveled from one bend, island, or other landmark in the river to the next.

❧ November 16, 1803

Lewis, Clark, a few other men, and Seaman crossed to the western side of the Mississippi in a pirogue. While exploring the forest they found an Indian camp. The Indians had never seen a Newfoundland, a dog as big as a small black bear. One Indian offered to buy Seaman. Lewis refused and that night wrote in his journal, "one of the Shawnees a respectable looking Indian offered me three beverskins for my dog with which he appeared much pleased, the dog was of the newfoundland breed one that I prised much for his docility and qualifications generally for my journey and of course there was no bargan, I had given 20$ for this dogg myself."

No, Seaman was not for sale. He had already proved his usefulness, and the men knew the dog would be a valuable ally as the expedition reached more dangerous territory. Four days later the bows of the pirogues and the keelboat faced upstream, and the men began to pull their oars against the Mississippi's strong current. The Corps of Discovery would be battling the power of the Mississippi, then of the Missouri, until they reached that river's source in the far-away, mysterious Rocky Mountains.

Chapter
2

———◆———

Up the Missouri

In the winter of 1803–1804, people in St. Louis grew accustomed to the sight of Captain Meriwether Lewis and his giant black dog hurrying along the muddy, slushy streets. Then, of course, St. Louis was not a large city with a population of a half million, as it is today. It was a small frontier town of a thousand people, many of French descent. Nevertheless, St. Louis was a vital center in the fur trade of the western frontier and a source of both supplies and information needed by the Corps of Discovery.

The expedition had made a winter camp by a little river—the Dubois or Wood River—that flowed into the Mississippi about eighteen miles north of St. Louis. To the northwest the men could see the Missouri River flowing into the Mississippi. Both were mighty rivers whose powerful currents carried uprooted trees and other hazards to boats. As the expedition struggled up the Mississippi in the fall of 1803, Lewis and Clark agreed that they would need more men in order to make faster progress upstream.

William Clark usually stayed at the camp by the Wood River.

The men addressed both Clark and Lewis as "Captain" and considered the two equal in rank. They never learned that the War Department had given Clark the lower rank of lieutenant, a decision that upset Lewis, who believed strongly that the leaders should be of equal rank. As co-captains they worked remarkably well together. The matter of Clark's unequal rank was not corrected until the year 2000, when President William Jefferson Clinton promoted Clark from lieutenant to captain.

On December 13, 1803, he wrote, "Set the Men to Clearing land & Cutting Logs." The men then built a small fort, comprised of several cabins enclosed by a stockade fence. It was mainly Clark's task to train the men for the journey ahead. Most of those who were not already in the army were required to enlist in order to be paid as soldiers.

Though they hunted for food and had other chores, the men were frustrated by the inactivity of winter camp. Fights broke out. Some men disobeyed orders and were punished. Some lost their chance to become members of the expedition, although, as it turned out, such men as John Colter and Reubin Field, who were often disciplined that winter, proved to be among the Corps' most trustworthy members.

One task that occupied the men was improving the keelboat. Clark had storage lockers built along the sides of the boat. When the wooden tops of the lockers were raised, they formed shields that could protect the boatmen from arrows and bullets. Clark also mounted a small cannon on the keel-boat's bow. He took these steps because both he and Lewis were worried about trouble with Indians. Fur traders who had journeyed partway up the Missouri warned them about the Sioux, who sometimes robbed river travelers or forced them to turn back.

In St. Louis, Meriwether Lewis learned as much as possible about the Indians and the Missouri River. He obtained maps that traced the river's path to the settlement of the Mandan Indians, a trading center in present-day North Dakota. Lewis and Clark hoped to reach the Mandan before winter.

As spring advanced, the men were raring to go. In preparation for leaving, Lewis and Clark promoted three men to sergeants. These men were asked to keep journals, too, in case the captains' journals were lost or damaged.

⇛ May 14, 1804

While Meriwether Lewis completed the last of his obligations in St. Louis, Clark set out from Camp Wood. On May 14 the keelboat and two pirogues "proceeded on under a jentle breese up the Missourie" for a few miles, to the village of St. Charles.

⇛ May 21, 1804

Lewis joined the men on May 20. With him were some St. Louis residents, who together with the villagers stood on the northern shore of the Missouri and cheered as the three boats set out on the rainy afternoon of May 21.

This night the expedition made camp on an island. A

hard rain fell. It was difficult to keep a fire for cooking going, but the rain did not dampen the men's spirits. Listening to their voices, Seaman could sense their excitement about finally being underway. There would be no more fresh supplies from stores. They

were on their own, and from this date onward, each day would carry them farther away from civilization.

➤ May 24, 1804

The heavily loaded keelboat was difficult to handle in the Missouri River's swift waters. In addition to as many as twenty-two men powering oars, others sometimes pulled on a tow rope from shore. They had to stay alert; sometimes a section of undermined shoreline suddenly collapsed into the river. On this day Clark wrote, "the Violence of the Current was so great that the Toe roap Broke, the Boat turned Broadside, as the Current Washed the Sand from under her She wheeled & lodged on the bank below as often as three times."

Time and again the crew saved the unwieldy boat from tipping over and spilling its precious cargo. Sometimes the men also had to avoid whole clumps of uprooted trees that rushed downstream. The smaller pirogues were more maneuverable than the keelboat. All three craft had masts and sails and when in deep water could take advantage of favorable winds. But too often the crews had to use iron-tipped poles to push the boats through shallow areas. It was slow going, and the expedition gained only about ten miles a day.

Each day Clark carefully noted distance traveled, compass directions, and details about islands in the Missouri and streams that entered it. Later he would use this information to make the first finely detailed map of the Missouri River and its surroundings. Each day several men left the boats to hunt for food. They brought back deer, wild turkeys, and other animals as well as observations about the countryside that were recorded in journals.

A life-size statue at Great Falls, Montana, shows Lewis holding his espontoon.

About six feet long, an espontoon had a metal blade on one end that could be used as a spear and walking stick. Near its top it had a small platform on which to rest a rifle barrel, to help achieve a steady aim, which was difficult with the expedition's heavy flintlock rifles.

With a rifle over his shoulder and Seaman at his side, Meriwether Lewis also explored the land and its life. Being the only person on the expedition trained as a scientist, he was as likely to return with mineral and plant specimens as he was with a dead turkey. Each dawn as the men prepared to launch the boats, Seaman waited eagerly for signs that Lewis was staying on land. If Lewis picked up his rifle and his espontoon—a kind of combination spear and walking stick—Seaman wagged his tail with excitement at the prospect of a day ashore full of new sights, sounds, and smells.

⇘ June 5, 1804

Day after day the men ate mostly meat. They craved more variety in their diet. On this day York swam to a sandbar to gather green edible plants, including water-cress, for dinner.

On this date also, Clark wrote, a scout discovered the fresh sign of about ten Indians. Although the native people of the area (present-day Missouri) were friendly, the captains ordered men to take turns standing guard at night. The guards could usually count on Seaman's keen sense of hearing and smell to warn of danger.

In the daytime, too—in camp, in a boat, or while exploring inland—the men came to rely on the big dog's extraordinary senses. They learned to pay attention to Seaman as they would to any exceptional guard or scout. Seaman usually heard the sounds of hunters returning to camp long before the men did. The members of the expedition also learned to pay attention to different tones of the dog's voice. Sometimes Seaman's barks warned of danger, perhaps a rattlesnake among the rocks near camp.

Within the human nose are 10 million nerve cells (neurons) that detect odors. Within the nose of a Newfoundland and most other breeds of dog are as many as 200 million neurons. This enables dogs to detect many more scents than humans and also to concentrate on one faint odor out of many, such as that of a person. Dogs rely on their sense of smell so much that the largest part of their brains is devoted to interpreting smells. A dog's sense of hearing is also more sensitive than that of humans and covers a wider range of sounds.

✤ June 16, 1804

"the Boat . . . assended the middle of the Streem which was diffucult Dangerious We Came to above this place at Dark and Camped in a bad place, the misquitoes and Ticks are noumerous & bad."

✤ June 24, 1804

"the Musquitors Ticks & Knats verry troublesom." Clark wrote frequently about pests. The men had mosquito netting that offered some protection in their tents at night, and they smeared animal grease on exposed skin as a kind of insect repellent. Most of these pests were less trouble for Seaman, thanks to his long thick hair. His hair was shortest on his face and ears, and that is where mosquitoes and ticks tried to settle down. Attached ticks were sometimes plucked off by Lewis or others in the evenings.

⇾ June 27–29, 1804

The expedition paused for several days where the Kansas River flows into the Missouri (near present-day Kansas City). This was a welcome break from the upstream struggles but was far from a rest stop. The men repaired a pirogue and the keelboat's tow rope. They prepared deerskins to be made into pants and shirts. They spread out supplies, including gunpowder, to dry in the sun and made sure their rifles were in good working order.

Hunters set out in different directions. On June 28 Clark wrote, "our hunters Killed Several Deer and Saw Buffalow." The men had seen tracks and other signs of bison before but this was the first sighting of the animal itself.

There was no way to preserve meat well, but the flesh of deer, elk, and other animals was "jerked"—cut in thin strips and dried in the sun. The dried strips, called jerky, were a common travel ration on the frontier.

⇾ July 5, 1804

July 4 had been the twenty-eighth birthday of the United States. After gaining fifteen miles upriver, the men had camped by a good-sized creek that flowed into the Missouri,

On July 4, 1804 William Clark recorded compass readings and miles traveled, and also wrote "Jos: Fields got bit by a Snake, which was quickly doctored with Bark by Cap Lewis."

The men on this expedition have been called the "writingest explorers of all time." The journals kept by Lewis, Clark, and some of the sergeants are a rich source of information—about wildlife, other resources, Indian customs. Still, there are puzzling gaps. For example, no writings by Lewis in the spring and summer of 1804 have been found. This is a great loss because Meriwether Lewis was the best writer of the group and the only one with scientific training.

naming it Independence Creek. They fired the keelboat's cannon in honor of Independence Day, and everyone was given an extra ration of whiskey.

The next day they struggled to gain ten miles as they passed through an area of treacherous sandbars. They had left forests behind and were now passing through prairie. The riverbanks and creek valleys were still lined with trees, however, and beavers were plentiful. The men sometimes hunted beavers, not only for their prized fur but also as a source of tasty food.

The boats came ashore near a beaver lodge. Judging from the freshly cut tree limbs that had been added to the giant wooden structure, the lodge appeared to be occupied by several beavers. The men called Seaman and urged him to get the beavers out. He plunged into the river and dived down to the entrance of the lodge. Soon a beaver swam up to the surface—then another. Several rifles fired, and Seaman retrieved the beavers, bringing them to shore. That night he was fed some of the fine food he had helped obtain.

⇻ July 14, 1804

Captain Clark and George Drouillard shot at three elk on the shore. The elk ran into the river. Seaman leaped into the water and swam after them, but the elk did not seem to be wounded, so Seaman was called back to the boat. He clambered aboard, with a helping hand, and gave some oarsmen a welcome shower as he shook the water off his coat.

⇻ July 19, 1804

The farther from civilization the expedition traveled, the more opportunities the men had to give names to creeks and other features of the landscape. On this day William Clark chose a peculiar name for a small island. "I call this Island Butter Island, as at this place we mad use of the last of our butter."

The expedition was in no danger of running out of more basic necessities, such as gunpowder and ink. Some evenings Lewis and Clark only had time to scribble some notes about the day's progress, events, and discoveries. Other times they spent hours at their small collapsible desks, catching up, writing in more detail. As Meriwether Lewis wrote by candlelight, Seaman often lay at his feet, lulled to sleep by the scratching sound of a quill pen on paper.

⇻ July 30, 1804

On this day Joseph Field shot a strange-looking animal. Clark described it as having the shape and size of a beaver, the mouth and head of a dog with its ears cut off, and the tail and hair of a groundhog. It was a badger, a new creature to

Badger

the men and to Seaman, who inhaled its distinctive scent. Lewis skinned the badger and preserved it for sending back to President Jefferson.

❧ August 12, 1804

Resting on the deck of the keelboat, Seaman was startled to hear a bark. He leaped up and stared intently at an animal on shore. It had an unmistakably doglike shape. Seaman growled. It was a coyote, which Clark called a prairie wolf.

The coyote got away, but in recent days the men had successfully collected specimens of other creatures that were new to them: least tern, pelican, bull snake. Lewis took measurements and made detailed descriptions in his journal.

❧ August 19, 1804

Seaman nuzzled Sergeant Floyd's hair and licked his hand. Charles Floyd gave the dog's head a weak pat. He was very sick, and the medicine Captain Lewis gave him did not help. All of the men, and especially York, were attentive to him.

The next day, after twelve miles of rowing, the expedition landed on the east side of the Missouri. They built a fire and began to heat kettles of water to give Floyd a warm bath, "hopeing it would brace him a little." But Floyd said, "I am going away" and died.

Charles Floyd was buried on top of a hill that overlooked the Missouri River. The captains named the hill Sergeant Floyds Bluff and a nearby stream Floyds River. That night the men camped by Floyds River, probably feeling both sad and worried. No one knew why Charles Floyd had died. So far during their journey nearly everyone, including Meriwether Lewis, had felt sick from time to time but had recovered. Would Floyd's mysterious sickness strike again? Would the men need to dig other graves?

Floyd may have died of infection from a ruptured appendix. He would have died even if he had been in Philadelphia, where most of the nation's best doctors resided, because this disease was not understood until decades later. Floyd died near present-day Sioux City, Iowa.

❧ August 23, 1804

Seaman had smelled the odor of bison while exploring with Lewis, but on this day he inhaled the scent at close range. Joseph Field came to the shore and shouted that he had shot a bison. Lewis ordered a dozen men to help butcher it and bring it to shore farther upstream. That night the men and the dog feasted on a new kind of meat. They found bison by the thousands farther upriver, and bison meat became a common food for the expedition.

❧ August 25, 1804

The captains, several men, and Seaman set out to visit a rise of land called the Mountain of Spirits, a site the Indians considered sacred. After walking four miles they crossed a creek and proceeded on. Though cloudy, the day was hot and humid—trying conditions for Seaman in his shaggy black coat. Clark wrote, "at two miles further our Dog was So Heeted & fatigued we was obliged Send him back to the Creek." Seaman flopped down in the water with only his head exposed and drank deeply. After reaching and exploring the mound, several of the men also complained of great thirst and hurried back to the creek.

⤞ September 1, 1804

The expedition camped for the night on the downstream shore of an island. The men often spent the night on islands, which offered protection from sneak attacks. So far they had seen little sign of Indians. Some tribes had been greatly reduced in number by the disease smallpox, and the Indians usually traveled westward in the summer, hunting where bison were most abundant.

Each day the men shot several deer, elk, bison, and other animals in order to provide everyone with meat. Wild berries, grapes, plums, and other fruit were plentiful, and so were fish. Clark wrote, "it is not necessary to mention fish as we catch them at any place on the river."

⤞ September 7, 1804

In recent days Seaman had sniffed deeply of scents arising from fresh tracks on the plains. The odors were new to him. Captain Clark wrote of fleet "wild goats"—pronghorns—and deer with black tails—mule deer. Both mammals were also new to the men of the expedition.

The boats set out in the chilly dawn, and rowed upriver about five and a half miles. They landed near the base of a dome-shaped hill that the captains wanted to climb. Views from high places helped them make observations in their journals about the land and wildlife beyond the river's course.

Descending the hill, Lewis and Clark came upon a village

of small burrowing animals that French fur traders had mentioned. The fur traders called them petite chiens— little dogs.

As the men became acquainted with the black-tailed prairie dog, they observed other wildlife, including rattlesnakes and coyotes, that hunted these animals. They killed a rattlesnake and found the remains of a prairie dog in its stomach.

In their journals the captains called them ground rats, barking squirrels, or prairie dogs. In the days ahead, vast colonies of these rodents would become a common sight, but the first sight of them made the men curious. Clark wrote in his journal that the animals "Set erect make a Whistleing noise and whin allarmed Slip into their hole."

Seaman rushed from one burrow to another, but the prairie dogs dashed underground before he could catch them. He inhaled the scent of a prairie dog that one of the men had shot. Meriwether Lewis wanted a live animal and ordered the men to dig into a burrow to catch one. As the spades dug deeper and deeper into the hard clay soil, Seaman waited nearby, ready to pounce on a fleeing prairie dog. Six feet down the men probed with sticks and figured they were only halfway to the bottom of the prairie dog's den.

They decided to try a new tactic. Two men stood guard by the boats while the others carried buckets of water from the river to the prairie dog colony. They poured up to five barrels of water into several burrows without success, but finally a wet and bedraggled prairie dog emerged and was

put in a cage. The prairie dog huddled in one corner of the cage when Seaman poked the tip of his nose into the other side. Lewis called his dog away. He had big plans for this prairie dog, captured in present-day Nebraska. He hoped to send it all the way back East to President Jefferson.

✺ September 10, 1804

On the top of a ridge several men gathered around some animal remains—a forty-five-foot-long backbone, several ribs, and teeth. They talked excitedly about the discovery. Seaman sniffed the bones without interest, except for one place where a male coyote had left its scent mark the night before. The bones were made of rock. They were the fossil remains of a plesiosaur—a giant swimming reptile that lived many million of years ago.

In the next few days Seaman found odors and tastes, that he found much more interesting. Captain Clark shot the expedition's first pronghorn (which the journal-keepers usually called wild goat or antelope). John Shields killed a "hare of the prairie"—a white-tailed jackrabbit. And on another day a black-billed magpie—another animal that was new to science—was collected. Lewis took careful measurements, wrote detailed descriptions, and often made drawings of new animals in his journal.

Plesiosaurs were long-necked reptiles with small heads and paddle-shaped legs that propelled them through the water— including the shallow seas that once covered large areas of what is now the central United States. Scientists in the early 1800s were puzzled by discoveries of huge fossil skeletons; the word dinosaur *was not coined until 1841.*

❧ September 15, 1804

The Missouri led northwest, and the calendar led toward autumn. In the evening Clark wrote, "this evening is verry Cold" and a "Great many wolves of Different Sorts howling about us."

By now Seaman had grown somewhat accustomed to the calls of coyotes and wolves, but he never lost interest in the sounds of these wild canines, his distant relatives.

❧ September 20, 1804

The captains chose to camp on a large sandbar in the river. Eventually everyone fell asleep except one guard, who tended the campfire and listened to a distant coyote chorus and the steady flow of the Missouri. Then he began to hear splashing sounds at the sandbar's edge. He discovered that the sandbar was being undermined and washed away by rising water. He yelled for the captains.

By moonlight Clark saw that the land both below and above the camp was rapidly falling into the river. He ordered everyone to load the boats and push off into the river as quickly as possible. By the time they reached the shore they could see that their entire campsite had been swallowed up by the Missouri.

⇶ September 23, 1804

As they rowed upstream, one of the men saw smoke rising from downstream. They were concerned because Indians sometimes set prairie fires as signals, and the boats were now in the territory of the powerful Teton Sioux. Sure enough, that afternoon three boys from the Teton Sioux tribe swam across to the expedition's camp. Two Sioux villages lay ahead, and the boys had set the fire to alert those camps of the boats' approach. Lewis and Clark gave the boys tobacco for their chiefs and warriors and told them to invite the members of their tribe to meet the expedition at the mouth of the next river.

⇶ September 24, 1804

The men reached the meeting place (now called the Bad River, near present-day Pierre, South Dakota) by afternoon. Their camp was well guarded and alert. So far the expedition's meetings with Indians had been friendly enough. Lewis and Clark had met with chiefs of the Otoe tribe in mid-August and with the Yankton Sioux in late August. They had been warned repeatedly, though, about the Teton Sioux. Also, they had a communication problem. Their best interpreter of the Sioux language, Pierre Dorion, had stayed behind with the Yankton Sioux; he would eventually accompany some of their leaders to Washington, D.C. Now the corps' interpreters were Pierre Cruzatte, who knew only a little Sioux, and Drouillard, who knew sign language.

❧ September 25, 1804

The men set up an awning for shade, unpacked gifts, and finally dressed in their full military uniforms. About fifty Teton Sioux arrived, including three chiefs. Gifts of meat were exchanged. Meriwether Lewis wanted to give a speech he had prepared for all the Indian groups about how President Jefferson—"the Great Father"—desired trade and peaceful relations with all Native Americans. For lack of a good interpreter, however, he cut the speech short and gave gifts and medals to the chiefs.

Lewis judged that one chief, Black Buffalo, was the leader and that the other two, Partisan and Buffalo Medicine, were lesser chiefs. He gave Black Buffalo a red military coat, a hat, and a medal. The others received only medals and a few small items—a mistake, since the three were of equal rank.

The gifts to different tribes varied but always included silver peace medals for the chiefs. An image of President Jefferson was engraved on one side; a handshake and the words "Peace and Friendship" were shown on the other. Lewis urged chiefs to turn in similar medals they might have received from other nations that claimed land in North America.

Partisan, in particular, was upset at this slight.

The chiefs were invited aboard the keelboat, anchored offshore, where Seaman had been confined for safekeeping. They were given a small drink of whiskey but "Soon began to be troublesom," and Clark ordered seven men to take the chiefs to shore in a pirogue. Warriors seized the boat's line and mast. Partisan demanded a canoe-load of presents before the expedition could go on.

Clark drew his sword and signaled the men to prepare for battle. Loaded rifles and the keelboat's cannon were aimed toward shore. Some Sioux warriors backed away but others pulled arrows from their quivers and prepared to fire.

Had one arrow been shot or one bullet been fired, the course of history would have changed. Many Sioux would have died, but they greatly outnumbered the men of the expedition and could shoot their arrows much faster than the men could reload their rifles. Any survivors of the Corps of Discovery would have retreated downriver.

Black Buffalo stepped forward, took the pirogue's bowline, and ordered his men away from the boat. As best he could through the interpreters, Clark spoke forcefully about the expedition's strength, saying that it "must and would go on." He offered to shake hands but was refused.

As Clark waded back to the pirogue, Black Buffalo and two of his warriors asked to sleep on the keelboat. Clark allowed this. The boats proceeded upriver a mile and anchored for the night near a small island. Clark wrote, "I call this Island bad humered Island as we were in a bad humer."

⇥ September 26, 1804

The boats proceeded upriver about four miles to Black Buffalo's village. The chief seemed genuinely interested in peace and invited Lewis to stay for a few days. With Seaman by his side, the captain walked among the tepees with Black Buffalo. The Teton Sioux were fascinated with the big Newfoundland dog, which to them seemed more bear than dog. Seaman was uneasy, surrounded as he was by hundreds of strangers and by Indian dogs. He sniffed cautiously at the dogs, and they at him, but his size and some deep growls kept the dogs at a respectful distance.

Indian dogs of the Great Plains resembled wolves and were sometimes used to haul heavy loads. Dogs west of the Rockies were smaller and had short hair. They were used to hunt elk. Just as the languages and customs of Native Americans varied, so did their attitudes about dogs. Tribes of the plains served dog meat on special occasions, while those of the Far West rejected the idea of dogs as food.

On this and the next evening the men were treated to feasts of buffalo, ground potatoes, and dog. The Teton Sioux often served roasted dog to honored guests. The Sioux also performed a scalp dance. Many of the scalps they held aloft on sticks were fresh, taken in a recent battle with Omaha Indians.

47

From that battle the Teton Sioux held forty-eight Omaha women and children as prisoners. Cruzatte, who spoke Omaha, was told by these captives that the Sioux intended to stop the expedition and rob it. The captains cautioned everyone to be on guard.

Late in the evening of September 27, Lewis and Clark were accompanied to their pirogue by Partisan and a warrior. Lewis stayed on shore with a guard while Clark was ferried to the keelboat. By accident the pirogue slammed into the keelboat's anchor cable and broke it. The big boat began to swing in the current. Clark yelled, alerting everyone to get to their oars.

Partisan was alarmed by the sudden activity and the shouting in words he did not understand. The Sioux were worried about a surprise raid by the Omaha, and Partisan jumped to the conclusion that this was what was happening. He yelled for help, and soon about two hundred Sioux warriors were at the riverbank. Fortunately, Black Buffalo was there, too, and helped restore calm.

Lacking its anchor, the men tied the keelboat to a tree by the riverbank—a vulnerable position. Clark wrote, "we kept a Strong guard all night in the boat no Sleep."

❧ September 28, 1804

Much of the morning was spent searching in vain for the anchor, which had been swallowed by sand and mud. The men were eager to be underway, but they were delayed once more when Teton Sioux warriors grabbed the keelboat's bowline and demanded tobacco. After some tense moments and some shouting, the men threw a few twists of tobacco leaves onto the shore. Black Buffalo yanked the line from the warriors, and the keelboat was free.

With great relief the Corps of Discovery pulled away from the Teton Sioux villages. They camped on the safest place they could find—a small sandbar in the middle of the river.

❧ September 30, 1804

Yesterday the expedition advanced eleven and a half miles upriver. On this day the explorers were underway at daybreak, hoisting sails to catch a wind from the south and gained twenty miles for the day. Each mile put the near-disaster with the Teton Sioux farther behind, and the men began to relax.

❧ October 20, 1804

On this day Meriwether Lewis wrote that Pierre Cruzatte "shot at a white bear he wounded him, but being alarmed at the formidable appearance of the bear he left his tomahalk and gun." Cruzatte later retrieved his dropped weapons, but the bear was not found. This was the expedition's first encounter with a grizzly bear.

About two weeks after leaving the Teton Sioux, the men paused for four days near a large island encampment of the Arikara—an agricultural tribe that grew corn, beans, and squash. The Arikara population had been greatly reduced by a smallpox epidemic. Lewis and Clark met with Arikara chiefs, gave them gifts, and told them about their "father," President Jefferson. As was their custom they also offered the chiefs a drink of whiskey. The Arikaras refused, expressing surprise that their father would give them liquor that would make them fools.

❧ October 21, 1804

Snow began to fall at dawn. Seaman smelled it, frisked around in it, rolled in it. He had not played in snow since March in faraway Pittsburgh. His undercoat hairs were growing, becoming more dense, becoming a winter coat that in the coming season would keep him much warmer than the men.

⇨ October 25, 1804

The expedition had made good progress in the autumn, often helped by a southerly wind pushing against the sails. Some days, however, gaining just a few miles was a struggle: "river full of Sand bars & we are at a great loss to find the Channel of the river, frequently run on the Sand bars which Detain us much."

⇨ October 27, 1804

As the men neared the Mandan villages, they sometimes paused to speak with groups of Mandan Indians on shore. The Mandan had long been friendly to white traders, some of whom lived among them. The boats landed on the south (or west) side of the Missouri River near two villages. The captains sent gifts of tobacco to the Mandan chiefs and invited them to meet. Once again Seaman attracted attention—from the Indians and their dogs as he walked beside Lewis. The captain kept him close.

⇨ October 29, 1804

Meriwether Lewis gave his formal speech to the Mandan chiefs (this time with a good interpreter). The Mandan were pleased that the men of the expedition would be neighbors for the winter.

The Mandan lived in two villages, and their allies the Hidatsa lived in three villages on the nearby Knife River (near present-day Bismarck, North Dakota). Nearly four thousand people lived in the villages—about four times the population of St. Louis. More than eight hundred of the Mandan and Hidatsa were warriors and could have quickly snuffed out the Corps of Discovery. However, they had good reasons to foster friendly relations with the newcomers. Their villages were the trading center of the Northern Plains, visited by several far-flung Indian tribes and by traders from St. Louis and from British territory to the north. Some French and English traders lived among the Mandan.

The Mandan lived in large round lodges, with walls and domed roofs made of mud and grasses spread over a framework of branches. Each lodge was big enough for several families and even for their horses, which were tied inside near the entrance.

❧ November 2, 1804

A few days earlier Captain Clark and a group of men explored upriver several miles but failed to find a suitable place for a winter camp. On this day a fine wooded site was found downstream. (A plentiful supply of trees was needed for building cabins.) Construction began right away. The fort was roughly the shape of a triangle, with two rows of huts forming two sides. It had outer stockade walls eighteen feet tall. The captains called their winter home Fort Mandan in honor of their friendly neighbors.

❧ November 6, 1804

After midnight the guard awakened the captains to come see the spectacle of the northern lights. Seaman was at Lewis's side. He had come along eagerly but could neither smell nor hear any animal or other thing that would account for the excitement in the men's voices. He sat quietly as they exclaimed about streaks and columns of colored light that danced above the northern horizon.

✣ December 7, 1804

Although it was not yet officially winter, deep cold descended on the Northern Plains. Ice covered the Missouri River. The Mandan chief named Big White invited members of the expedition to join in hunting a large herd of buffalo discovered in the area. Captain Lewis and fifteen men, riding borrowed Indian horses, killed fourteen bison. However, darkness fell before they were able to haul all of the meat back to the fort.

"all meat which is left out all night falls to the Wolves which are in great numbers . . . three men frost bit badly to day," Clark wrote.

✣ December 17, 1804

This morning the thermometer stood at 45 degrees below zero Fahrenheit. Seaman spent many hours indoors napping but never slept close to the fire. His full winter coat kept him comfortable. Seaman was not allowed to roam far at night. Despite his size and strength, he would be no match for a pack of hungry wolves.

❧ December 25, 1804

In celebration of Christmas the keelboat cannon—now mounted on the fort—was fired three times as the flag was raised at dawn. All of the men and the dog ate well. Seaman kept out of the way as Pierre Cruzatte played his fiddle and the men danced jigs and square dances. The celebration lasted until late—9 P.M.

Before the invention of electric light bulbs, people went to bed much earlier than they do today. The explorers were often underway at dawn and worked hard, so 9 P.M. was not an unusual bedtime.

The expedition settled in for the winter. Seaman slept a lot and greeted the many Mandan who visited the fort. The captains caught up on journal-writing while the others hunted for food and firewood, repaired equipment, and made clothes and moccasins from animal skins. They sang songs and sometimes played the game of backgammon.

The Corps of Discovery, halfway to the Pacific Ocean, was safe and warm for the winter.

Chapter
3

Into Uncharted
Territory

SEAMAN PRANCED WITH EXCITEMENT as the men loaded boats on the northern shore of the Missouri. It was April 7, 1805, and the Corps of Discovery was leaving Fort Mandan.

Leaping aboard the keelboat, the big dog inhaled the scent of the prairie dog in its cage. Then Seaman sniffed at the cages of the birds—four magpies and a prairie grouse—that had also been put on the keelboat. This live cargo was only a small part of the treasure that was being sent down the Missouri and on to President Jefferson. Lewis and Clark had carefully labeled and bundled up dried plant specimens, minerals, and the skins and skeletons of several mammals, including a male and female pronghorn.

Even more important were their written report to the president, letters, and a map that William Clark had drawn. It showed the United States west of the Mississippi. The map was based on Clark's compass readings and skilled estimates of miles traveled along the Missouri, but it also included information he had gained from the Native Americans along the way. Clark had spent many winter hours asking the Mandan and Hidatsa about the upper Missouri River and its tributaries. Hidatsa war parties roamed far to the west, so they were a vital source of information about a vast territory unknown to any white man.

About 4 P.M. there was a flurry of handshakes and good-byes. Corporal Richard Warfington stroked Seaman's fur as he listened to Captain Lewis's final instructions. Then the bow of the keelboat and one small canoe swung downstream as Warfington and eleven men set out for St. Louis.

The live animals, journals, and other items journeyed down the Missouri and the Mississippi to New Orleans, then went by sailing ship to Baltimore, finally arriving in Washington, four months later, in August 1805. One magpie and the prairie dog reached Jefferson alive. The prairie dog lived in the East for several months, with its remarkable life ending at the Peale Museum in Philadelphia.

Soon after the keelboat's flashing oars disappeared around a bend, the Corps of Discovery launched their boats—the two pirogues and six new canoes the men had hewn from cottonwood trees. As Meriwether Lewis had planned long ago, the expedition now included himself; his dog; his fellow leader, William

Clark; Clark's slave, York; and a force of well-trained and eager men—three sergeants and twenty-three privates. It also included hunter and interpreter George Drouillard and another interpreter who had lived among the Hidatsa, the French Canadian Toussaint Charbonneau.

Lewis, however, had never imagined the last two members of the expedition: the teenage mother Sacagawea and her two-month-old infant son. About sixteen, Sacagawea had already led a remarkable life. A Shoshone, she was about twelve when she and another girl were taken prisoner by a Hidatsa war party. Later, back at the Hidatsa village, Charbonneau had bought the two Shoshone teenagers as wives.

After their troubles with the Teton Sioux, Lewis and Clark recognized the value of having an interpreter who spoke the language of the Shoshone, who lived far up the Missouri in the mysterious Rocky Mountains. They gained that interpreter, Sacagawea, by hiring Charbonneau. Having Sacagawea and her baby along would also ease the fears of the Indians they met, since war parties were never accompanied by women and children.

Lewis had more medical knowledge than anyone else on the expedition. A woman's first delivery is often difficult, so Lewis gave a folk remedy to Sacagawea that was reputed to help. He broke up pieces of a rattlesnake's rattle into little bits and mixed them with water. Sacagawea gave birth less than ten minutes after drinking the mixture. Lewis wrote, "this remedy may be worthy of future experiments."

Several weeks earlier, on February 11, Meriwether Lewis had assisted Sacagawea as she gave birth to her son. The baby was named Jean Baptiste Charbonneau but was given the nickname Pompy or Pomp by William Clark. Most of the men were unmarried and hadn't much experience with babies, but they were pleased to have Pomp along. But Seaman was the most fascinated of all by Sacagawea's baby—a source of endlessly interesting scents and sounds. Seaman investigated Pomp several times a day, nuzzling and observing this tiny addition to the Corps of Discovery as it set forth into the unknown. Before the boats were launched upstream, Lewis wrote, "We were now about to penetrate a country at least two thousand miles in width, on which the foot of civillized man had never trodden."

Sacagawea

Meriwether Lewis wrote that the name Sacagawea meant Bird Woman. There is still uncertainty about the origin of her name and how it was pronounced. She was from the Lemhi Shoshone tribe but may have been given a Hidatsa name after she was taken prisoner. If that was the case, her name was probably pronounced "Chicago-wea."

⇥ April 8, 1805

This morning Lewis walked along the river with Seaman and paid a farewell visit to Black Cat, the Mandan chief. The men of the expedition had just endured the coldest winter of their lives and probably could not have survived without corn the Indians had grown and stored. They had obtained the corn by trading. Meriwether Lewis had been wise to include John Shields in his crew, for Shields was a skilled blacksmith. All through the winter he repaired tools, sharpened axes, and made hide scrapers and battle-axes in exchange for Mandan corn.

Lewis thought highly of Black Cat, and they parted as friends. With Seaman running ahead, Lewis returned to the shore and waited for the boats to arrive. The expedition paddled and rowed several miles upstream before making camp. On this night and for many nights to come, the men slept in the open under blankets or robes made of bison hides. A canvas tent was usually the sleeping quarters for the two captains, George Drouillard, Charbonneau, Sacagawea, the baby, and Seaman.

⇝ April 13, 1805

The captains ordered that the sails on the pirogues be hoisted to take advantage of a wind from the south. The white pirogue, slightly smaller than the red, was considered the more stable. It was loaded with the most precious cargo, including medicines, the best trade goods, and the captains' journals. Among the pirogue's six paddlers were three men who could not swim; this craft was considered the safest place for them. Sacagawea, with Pomp in a cradleboard on her back, was also aboard with her husband.

More than a thousand miles from its mouth, the Missouri was still wide, deep, and dangerous. A sudden wind squall nearly tipped the pirogue over. Charbonneau turned the rudder in the wrong direction, making matters worse. Lewis ordered Drouillard to take control of the rudder. The sails were then taken in, and the pirogue steadied itself. Had it overturned, Lewis later wrote, most of those aboard would have perished, "as the waves were high, and the perogue upwards of 200 yards from the nearest shore."

Exploring along the shore, Seaman began to growl. The hair along his back rose. The men found huge tracks of a white bear—a grizzly. Indians had warned them about the

The word grizzly *means "grayish or flecked with gray," so these bears are named for the gray or silver tips of their hairs. Lewis and Clark usually called them white bears. Indians warned them about these bears. Since the expedition had the best rifles then made, at first Lewis expected no trouble. But he underestimated grizzlies. Lewis and several other men narrowly escaped from grizzlies, sometimes by leaping into a river.*

grizzly: "this anamall is said more frequently to attack a man on meeting with him, than to flee from him," Lewis wrote.

⇝ April 18, 1805

A hunter shot a goose, and Seaman leaped into the river and swam back with the bird in his mouth. Seaman loved to ramble on the land with Captain Lewis, but time and again he had proved to be useful as a retriever, so he was sometimes kept aboard for that purpose.

⇝ April 22, 1805

Hiking beside the river in the evening, Lewis was closely followed by a bison calf that had been separated from its herd. Lewis thought the calf followed close to his heels because it was afraid of his dog, which to the calf probably resembled the wolves that often preyed on buffalo herds.

⇝ April 24, 1805

The winds were so strong and the waves so high that the expedition did not move. Everyone suffered from sore eyes, which may have been caused by wind-driven sand. "so penitrating is this sand that we cannot keep any article free from it; in short we are compelled to eat, drink, and breath it very freely," wrote Lewis.

At night the powerful winds from the north continued. Seaman wandered off and did not return. Lewis yelled his dog's name into the howling wind. He told the sentry to stay alert for Seaman's return in the night, but the dog did not come home. Many of the men went to bed with troubled thoughts about the missing dog.

❧ April 25, 1805

"my dog had been absent during the last night, and I was fearfull we had lost him altogether, however, much to my satisfaction he joined us at 8 Oclock this morning."

Seaman was hungry, unhurt, and unable to give any clues about his rare night away from camp. Later in the morning, Lewis took Seaman and several men along the south bank of the Missouri, looking for a river called the Yellowstone that emptied into the Missouri. Lewis shot a buffalo calf, and the men and Seaman had a hearty meal at midday. That night they camped by the Yellowstone.

❧ April 26, 1805

Captain Lewis sent Joseph Field on a day's exploration of the Yellowstone. Several pronghorns were seen swimming in the river near camp. Without prompting, Seaman leaped into the water after them. With powerful strokes he closed in on one. "Drowned & killed it and Swam to Shore with it," wrote Sergeant Ordway in his journal. The pronghorn's meat was part of a feast held at the junction of the Yellowstone and the Missouri, where the Corps of Discovery camped.

❧ April 29, 1805

This morning Lewis shot and killed a grizzly bear that chased him for seventy or eighty yards after it had been wounded. The bear was added to the evening menu. The men killed only what they needed for food, but a lot of meat was needed to feed thirty-two people and a large dog. Travel-ing through present-day Montana, they found an abundance of wildlife. Lewis observed, "we can scarcely cast our eyes in any direction without percieving deer Elk Buffaloe or Antelopes."

❧ May 5, 1805

Many of the bison, elk, and other animals the expedition encountered had never seen humans. While walking along the shore the men sometimes threw sticks or stones simply to drive these animals out of the way. Seaman chased and caught another pronghorn. Ordinarily a pronghorn can outrun any dog, but many of the hoofed grazing animals were in poor condition after a long, hard winter.

In the evening Seaman began to bark. He had spotted a huge grizzly bear on the sandy beach near camp. The bear was hit by ten rifle balls before it fell. Its meat was cooked, its hide was saved, and its fat was boiled and kept for later use.

A few days later Charbonneau used some bear grease as cooking oil to fry giant sausages he had made of buffalo meat, which Lewis called one of the greatest delicacies of the forest. However, many of the men were suffering from sores and illness caused by their nearly all-meat diet of the spring. Sacagawea provided some variety. She was good at finding edible roots, wild onions, and other vegetables.

❧ May 14, 1805

The expedition gained over sixteen miles—a good day— but evening brought near disaster. Men in two canoes at the rear of the boats saw a grizzly bear near shore. Six men landed. They readied their rifles, crept close to the huge bear, and fired. Wounded with six rifle balls, the bear chased the men toward the shore. The men reloaded and fired again, but the grizzly charged two men who were hidden among willows at the river's edge. They threw their rifles aside and jumped off a twenty-foot-high embankment into the water. The bear plunged into the river after them but was finally killed by a rifle shot from shore.

At the same time, trouble struck upstream. A powerful gust of wind caught the sail of the white pirogue and nearly tipped it over. Once again Charbonneau turned the rudder the wrong way. Both Lewis and Clark were on shore, about three hundred yards away, and could only shout helplessly into the wind as they watched waves flood the boat.

Charbonneau abandoned the rudder and began praying, but Pierre Cruzatte threatened to shoot him if he did not turn the rudder. Precious papers and packages from the pirogue's bow began to float away, but Sacagawea, at the stern, reached out and rescued them. Two men bailed out some of the water with kettles while Cruzatte and two others rowed the pirogue to shore. There the men bailed out the rest of the water and spread the cargo on the shore to dry.

Lewis wrote, "we thought it a proper occasion to console ourselves and cheer the sperits of our men." Everyone was given a drink of whiskey. The journal writers praised Cruzatte and Sacagawea.

⋙ May 17, 1805

"Capt. Clark narrowly escaped being bitten by a rattle-snake in the course of his walk. . . . we called this stream rattlesnake creek."

Lewis described this species of snake, now called the

prairie rattlesnake, which was new to science. The expedition continued to encounter reptiles, birds, mammals, and plants that had never before been collected or described.

⇝ May 19, 1805

Each day the boats were usually underway at dawn, with breakfast eaten later in the morning. This morning a thick fog delayed the start until 8 A.M. Once the expedition was underway, Clark explored on land while Lewis, with Seaman, stayed aboard the white pirogue. The other men walked along the shore and pulled the pirogues by tow ropes.

Beaver were abundant on the upper Missouri and after the expedition left Fort Mandan were an important food source. In the afternoon, as Lewis wrote later, "one of the party wounded a beaver, and my dog as usual swam in to catch it." With powerful strokes Seaman closed in on the beaver. It dove but Seaman quickly followed and grabbed it by a hind leg. Twisting around underwater, the beaver bit deeply into one of Seaman's back legs. Seaman let go of the beaver's leg, then clenched his powerful jaws around its neck. He surfaced and swam to shore with the beaver in his mouth.

When Seaman brought the beaver to the hunter who had shot it, the man saw blood on the dead beaver—and blood spurting from the dog's leg. He yelled for Captain Lewis, who came running. The beaver's teeth had severed an artery, and Seaman had already lost a lot of blood swimming back to shore.

He was bleeding to death.

Lewis quickly tied a deerskin cord around Seaman's leg

above the wound. The bleeding slowed but did not stop. Lewis squeezed the wound shut with his fingers and ordered the hunter to run to the white pirogue and fetch medical supplies and help.

York and several other men soon appeared. Seaman was still conscious but very weak. He lay quietly while one man held the wound shut and Lewis sewed tight stitches with needle and thread. The bleeding finally stopped.

Several men lifted Seaman gently onto a blanket and carried him to camp.

Seaman seemed barely alive. Lewis wrote in his journal, "it was with great difficulty that I could stop the blood; I fear it will yet prove fatal to him."

❧ May 20, 1805

A few of the men lost sleep last night, nursing the Newfoundland dog. To everyone's great relief, Seaman was still alive in the morning. Lewis, York, and Sacagawea tended to him, checking his wound and giving him water. A soft, shaded bed was arranged on the white pirogue for Seaman. During the day and evening all the explorers visited the big dog and offered gentle touches and words of encouragement. Seaman could barely lift his head, but he wagged his tail weakly.

❧ May 25, 1805

Seaman was nearly his old self, though Lewis did not yet allow him to go on long hikes. His appetite was back, and this evening the dog and the others ate meat of a new flavor: bighorn sheep. Clark and two hunters had killed three of these animals, which in his journal Lewis called ibex or big horn animals.

❧ May 26, 1805

Aiming to climb some steep hills to view the country ahead, Lewis left Seaman on the pirogue. "on arriving to the summit one of the highest points in the neighbourhood I thought myself well repaid for any labour; as from this point I beheld the Rocky Mountains for the first time . . . these points of the Rocky Mountains were covered with snow and the sun shone on it in such manner as to give me the most plain and satisfactory view."

Later, near camp after dark, Lewis stepped within five inches of a rattlesnake, "but being in motion I passed before he could probably put himself in a striking attitude and fortunately escaped his bite."

⇶ May 29, 1805

After a long day of struggling up the river, most of the explorers went to sleep soon after dark. Four cooking fires were burning low, and a sentry listened carefully for any unusual sounds from the rugged bluffs rising above the campsite. No one expected trouble to come from the Missouri.

A huge dark form rose out of the water. A bull bison had crossed from the opposite shore, and now it clambered over the white pirogue, where the captains were sleeping, and charged through camp at full speed. Its hooves landed within inches of the heads of several sleeping men. The sentry yelled an alarm, causing the panicked bison to change direction and narrowly miss trampling other men who were just awakening.

As the bison thundered toward the tent, Seaman lunged out of its entrance and began barking. He chased the bison, keeping right behind its flying hooves. "my dog saved us," Lewis wrote, "by causing him to change his course a second time, which he did by turning a little to the right, and was quickly out of sight, leaving us by this time all in an uproar . . . we were happy to find no one hirt."

❧ May 31, 1805

The journey up the Missouri had become more and more of a struggle. Sandy cliffs rose along each shore, forming a natural funnel for strong downstream winds. Sails were useless. The current grew more swift, and the men were forced to tow the boats. They cut their feet on sharp rocks and were sometimes in frigid water up to their armpits. The tow ropes, made of elkskin, often broke. Despite their hard labor, the men could not help but admire the spectacular landscape along the river, especially the sandstone formations known as the White Cliffs. Lewis called them "seens of visionary inchantment."

❧ June 2, 1805

At dusk the men made camp on the Missouri's south shore. Upstream and across the river was a disturbing sight: a large river entering the Missouri. This was puzzling because the Hidatsa had said that the next important landmark would be great waterfalls. They had not mentioned this joining of two rivers. Which river would lead them through the Rocky Mountains?

The Hidatsa probably did not intend to mislead the captains. They usually traveled by horse on plains trails that bypassed long stretches of the Missouri, so possibly they were unaware of the river entering from the north. For the same reason they did not know the extent of the Great Falls or how difficult a portage past the falls would be.

❧ June 3, 1805

In early June the expedition rested for more than a week at the junction of the two rivers—a welcome break, since many of the men had cut and bruised feet. The two rivers were examined, measured, and explored upstream a few miles. The south fork was 372 yards wide, and its waters were clear, running over a stony bed. The north fork was 200 yards wide, and its waters were brown, running over a muddy bottom.

Most of the sergeants and privates believed that the north fork was the Missouri, since it looked exactly like the waters they had struggled against for so many miles. The captains disagreed. They thought that the north fork must pass a great distance through open plains in order to pick up its brown, muddy color. They argued that the clear waters of the south fork showed that this river came directly from the Rockies. They knew, however, that a wrong decision might make them lose so much time that they would reach the Rockies when winter snows had made them impassable. In fact, Lewis wrote, it would "probably so dishearten the party that it might defeat the expedition altogether."

❧ June 8, 1805

Seaman had proved to be a valuable guard dog at night, alerting the camp when he smelled or heard a grizzly bear or some other danger. So he was left at camp with most of the expedition while Clark and five men explored the south fork and Lewis and six men followed the course of the north river.

Both groups had set out a few days earlier, on June 4. The walking was difficult, as the spines of prickly pear cactus pierced the thin-soled moccasins the men wore. Lewis's group hiked about eighty miles up the north fork before returning on June 8. The river's course kept heading mainly north, not west, and this reinforced Lewis's belief it was not the Missouri. He was so certain that he named it Maria's River, after a cousin.

Clark and his men had returned earlier after hiking up the south fork about forty miles, heading west. They discovered the largest prairie dog town they had ever seen. Joseph Field was chased and nearly caught by a grizzly bear, but shouts and shots from the others scared it away.

✹ June 11, 1805

Lewis and Clark concluded that the south fork was the Missouri. Nearly all of the men still disagreed, and the captains made a plan to test their choice. After hiding the red pirogue and some supplies where the two rivers joined, Clark would lead the expedition up the south fork while Lewis and a few men dashed ahead. If they found the great waterfalls reported by the Hidatsa, the Corps of Discovery would know that they were paddling up the Missouri.

Meriwether Lewis felt ill the morning he and four men set out and by evening he had a high fever. He soon felt much better after drinking a lot of bitter tea made from choke-cherry twigs.

✹ June 13, 1805

Lewis's group of explorers found it easier to walk across the plains than to follow every twist and turn of the river. This morning Lewis turned south to be closer to the river. He began to hear the sound of falling water and then saw "spray arrise above the plain like a collumn of smoke." Hurrying ahead, Lewis began to hear roaring water that could only come from the great falls of the Missouri. By noon he beheld "the grandest sight" of his life and apologized in his journal for being unable to truly describe the spectacular waterfalls.

❧ June 14–19, 1805

Lewis had sent Joseph Field to tell Clark that the expedition was indeed on the right river. He explored upstream, expecting to find a long quiet stretch of the Missouri above the falls. Instead he discovered another great waterfall, and another, and another—five in all in twelve miles of rapids and fast-flowing water. The Hidatsa had mentioned one waterfall. They had said that the expedition would be able to carry their boats and goods around the great falls in one day. Clearly it would take much longer and proved to be an extraordinary challenge.

While Lewis hurried upriver to find the Great Falls, Sacagawea became seriously ill. Her symptoms included fever, low pulse, irregular breathing, and pain in her abdomen. Clark cut her several times, causing loss of blood—a medical treatment of the time that did her no good. When Lewis rejoined the main expedition he gave her some medicines and also water from a sulphur spring, figuring that iron in the water would help. To the men's relief, Sacagawea recovered. Had she died they would have had to care for a four-month-old baby, besides losing their only Shoshone interpreter and a valuable and respected member of the expedition.

To lighten their load, the men left behind the white pirogue and some equipment and supplies, hiding them well. Their route along the south side of the Missouri's falls and rapids would total eighteen miles of rough, hilly country. But there was no other choice. "God or bad," Lewis wrote on June 16, "we must make the portage." Trees were scarce in the area, but the men found a big cottonwood twenty-two inches in diameter. They sawed wheels from it and made crude wagons for hauling the canoes and supplies.

After dark on June 19, as the men sat mending their moccasins by firelight, Seaman began barking excitedly. Lewis wrote that the dog "seemed extreemly uneasy which was unusual with him." Worried about an attack by Indians or a grizzly, Lewis ordered three men to investigate. They reported that the dog had been barking at a bison bull near the camp. Herds of bison often passed by, and those unfortunate enough to be caught in the Missouri's rapids were swept to their deaths.

✦ Late June, 1805

Bison carcasses along the shore attracted many grizzly bears. Several men, including Captain Lewis, had narrow escapes from grizzlies. On June 27 Lewis reported the killing of the largest grizzly so far. The beast's hind feet were nearly twelve inches across, and its pelt was as large as that of an ox. The captains were so concerned about grizzlies that they did not allow anyone to hunt or go on any errand alone.

Nightfall always made the explorers especially grateful that Seaman was part of the Corps of Discovery. On June 27 Lewis wrote "my dog seems to be in a constant state of alarm with these bear and keeps barking all night." The next night Lewis wrote that the bears "come close arround our camp every night but have never yet ventured to attack us and our dog gives us timely notice of their visits, he keeps constantly padroling all night."

Day after day the men hauled heavy loads over land where prickly pear cactus thrived. They put an extra layer of

deerskin in their moccasins, but even this was a poor defense against cactus spines. Soon every step was painful. The big Newfoundland dog also suffered. Every evening he spent hours licking his wounded toe pads.

The effort of hauling canoes and baggage overland was a great ordeal for the men. On June 23 Lewis wrote, "their fatiegues are incredible; some are limping from the soreness of their feet, others faint and unable to stand for a few minutes, with heat and fatiegue, yet no one complains, all go with cheerfullness."

❧ June 29, 1805

The practically treeless landscape offered little firewood and no shelter from the hailstorm that surprised the expedition on this date. The explorers ducked under canoes or covered their heads with other objects to protect themselves from the hailstones, most of which were as big as pigeon eggs. Some were as big as apples. Lewis reported that most of the men were "bleeding freely and complained of being much bruised."

The storm almost took the lives of William Clark, Charbonneau, Sacagawea, and her baby. They had taken shelter from the storm under some ledges in a ravine near one of the falls on the Missouri. It seemed to be a dry and safe place in the violent downpour. Then Clark heard a rushing sound coming from farther up the ravine. In the nick of time he realized that a raging torrent of floodwater was rolling down the ravine toward them. He yelled for everyone to climb.

Clark was soon up to his waist in water as he helped push Sacagawea, who was carrying Pomp, up the steep side of the ravine. As they clambered to safety on the plain, the ravine filled with fifteen feet of water. A firearm, some other equipment, and Pomp's cradleboard were lost.

It was a close call. Lewis wrote of the flood: "one moment longer & it would have swept them into the river just above the great cataract of 87 feet where they must have inevitably perished."

❧ July 15, 1805

"At 10 A.M. we once more saw ourselves fairly under way much to my joy," wrote Lewis as the expedition set out on the Missouri in eight heavily loaded canoes. The difficult portage past the Great Falls was over. Some men probably felt that nothing worse could lie ahead. They were wrong.

Toward the end of the day Seaman once again proved to be a useful member of the expedition. Near camp a hunter wounded a deer that ran into the river. Seaman leaped into the water, caught the deer, and brought it to shore. Deer meat was part of this night's dinner.

While the main group of men struggled to bypass the Missouri's rapids with the canoes, equipment, and baggage, Lewis and the others assembled the iron frame of a boat he had designed and had made in Virginia. The frame weighed about two hundred pounds, but covered with elkskins the craft would carry about four tons. However, there were no pine or other coniferous trees in that region, and therefore no pitch with which to seal edges and holes. Lewis and his crew tried a substitute made of charcoal, tallow, and buffalo fat, but the boat leaked and was left behind. Lewis wrote that he was "mortifyed," partly because this effort had delayed the expedition for four or five days. It was further delayed while the men made two large dugout canoes to replace the iron boat.

⤜ July 19–21, 1805

Progress up the Missouri was slow and laborious. The men often had to pull the canoes with tow ropes, damaging their feet by stepping on sharp-edged flint rocks and prickly pear thorns. These cacti grew so abundantly in the river valley that at some campsites it was difficult to find cactus-free places to lie down. One evening Clark reported that he had pulled seventeen cactus thorns from his feet by the light of the fire. And he wrote, "Musqutors verry troublesom."

On July 21 Seaman caught several wild geese, "as he frequently dose" wrote Captain Lewis. Great numbers of geese were seen on and near the river. They were undergoing their annual molt of feathers and could not fly.

❧ July 22–27, 1805

The days grew shorter and progress upriver harder. Adding to the troubles were the barbed seeds of needlegrass that penetrated moccasins and leggings. Lewis wrote that the seeds "give us great pain untill they are removed. my poor dog suffers with them excessively." Seaman licked and nibbled on his paws and legs. He was often kept aboard one of the canoes to spare him the ordeal of walking on land.

Clark, eager to find the Shoshone, had scouted miles ahead of the canoes without success. The men's spirits rose, however, when Sacagawea began to recognize the countryside. She said they were close to a place called the Three Forks where three rivers joined and where her people camped. It was there she had been taken prisoner by a Hidatsa war party.

On the morning of July 27, to everyone's relief, they reached the Three Forks, in the heart of Shoshone territory.

❧ July 29, 1805

The expedition paused at the Three Forks while the men made or repaired moccasins and clothing. William Clark also needed time to recover from illness. Nearly every member of the Corps of Discovery had been sick at one time or another, and now Clark had a high fever, chills, and pains in his muscles, not to mention bruised and bloody feet.

The captains agreed that the

The three rivers seemed to be of equal size, and all drained from the Rockies, so Lewis felt that none of them should be called the Missouri. Besides naming one for Jefferson, he called one river the Gallatin (in honor of the secretary of the treasury) and the other the Madison (in honor of the secretary of state). Unlike many of the rivers and other landmarks named by Lewis and Clark, these rivers have the same names today.

southwest or right-hand fork was the one to follow. Lewis named it the Jefferson River in honor of the president. Within a few days Clark felt better but had a painful boil on one ankle, so he led the main party with the canoes while Lewis and several men scouted miles ahead, searching with increased anxiety for the Shoshone.

➤ August 2, 1805

The river twisted and turned and shrank in breadth and depth. Advancing upstream became even more difficult. Lewis discovered that the river was so shallow he could wade across. Seaman, always eager to swim, welcomed the chance to paddle across at his side.

The expedition feasted on the fruits of summer: yellow currants, black gooseberries, and purple serviceberries. Lewis observed that there was snow on top of the mountains that rose parallel to the river, "while we in the valley are nearly suffocated with the intense heat of the midday sun; the nights are so cold that two blankets are not more than sufficient covering."

➤ August 6–9, 1805

The Jefferson River also forked, and the captains chose to proceed up the middle stream (which today is called the Beaverhead River because a nearby hill resembles the head of a swimming beaver). Sacagawea recognized the place, saying that the area was a summer retreat for her people and that the Shoshone should be found soon.

The river was so shallow in spots that a heavily laden canoe would not float. The men were tired and their morale was low. It was time to abandon the boats and proceed on land, but the men alone could not carry all of the trade goods and gear. They needed horses from the Shoshone.

On the morning of August 9, Lewis said good-bye to Seaman, running his fingers through the thick black hair on the dog's neck. Seaman was going to stay with the main group, where he would be safer and most valuable to the expedition. Then Lewis set out on foot with three men, determined to head upstream and west until he was somehow able to return with horses.

➢ August 11, 1805

Crossing a plain, Lewis saw a man on horseback about two miles away. He took a closer look through his telescope. The rider's clothing identified him as a Shoshone. At closer range Lewis made friendly signals. Apparently he had asked Sacagewea the Shoshone word for white man, but the Shoshone people had never seen white men and had no word for them. She gave him the word *ta-ba-bone*, which meant stranger. Shouting "stranger" to people who feared war parties from the east did not help: the Indian fled.

➢ August 12, 1805

Disheartened, Lewis and his crew kept hiking west. The stream they followed dwindled in size until one man, Hugh McNeal, planted one foot on each side and declared that he was "bestride the mighty & heretofore deemed endless Missouri." They climbed a ridge and discovered that it was part of the Continental Divide, which ran through the Rockies. Streams flowing east drained into the Missouri, then the Mississippi, and eventually the Gulf of Mexico. On the other side of the ridge water flowed west, eventually reaching the Pacific Ocean.

The view from the top of the ridge shattered any remaining dreams of an easy passage from one river system to the other. Looking west, Lewis may have hoped to see a gentle terrain with the broad Columbia River flowing toward the Pacific. Instead he saw more of the Rocky Mountains—a landscape of deep canyons and ranges of rugged, snowcapped peaks.

Lewis and the three others climbed down the steep western slope of the ridge. They found a creek running west and drank from it. Lewis wrote, "here I first tasted the water of the great Columbia river." He was correct; the water of that creek did eventually reach the Columbia, but that occurred hundreds of miles from where they stood.

❧ August 13, 1805

After hiking about ten miles, Lewis's group met three Shoshone women. Pleased with the beads and mirrors Lewis gave them, the women were leading him to their camp when sixty armed warriors rode up on horseback. Lewis lay down his rifle as a sign of peace, and the oldest woman spoke favorably about the white men with presents. At last the expedition had found the Lemhi Shoshone (called the Snake by tribes of the Great Plains). These Indians had the horses that the Corps of Discovery so desperately needed.

➢ August 14–16, 1805

Several days passed while Lewis waited for Clark and the main group with the canoes to come up the Jefferson River. Meanwhile, he learned that the Shoshone were eager to head for the plains to hunt bison; they were desperate for food. When Drouillard shot three deer on August 16, Lewis was astonished to see the Indians gobble down meat and organs raw. The Shoshone feared that Lewis was allied with the Blackfeet or other enemies from the east. At the same time that Lewis tried to allay their suspicions, he also aroused their curiosity. Through Drouillard's sign language Lewis informed them that they would soon meet a woman of their own tribe (Sacagawea), a man with red hair (Clark), and a man with black skin (York)!

➢ August 17, 1805

Lewis, his men, and many Shoshone had traveled east to meet Clark and the others. About noon all of the members of the Corps of Discovery were reunited. Seaman raced to greet his master. He barked with joy and leaped up to lick Lewis's face, ignoring the strange Indians all around who exclaimed over the huge black dog. As the day went on the Shoshone could not help but notice how close Seaman stayed to Lewis's side and how well he obeyed. Lewis wrote that they admired "the segacity of my dog."

Meanwhile, another extraordinary reunion was occurring. Sacagawea recognized another

Lewis described the Lemhi Shoshone as "frank, communicative, fair in dealing, generous with the little they possess, extreemly honest." However, they were not fools and traded some of their poorest horses for items they prized, especially weapons to protect themselves against raids by better-armed tribes. On August 29 Clark exchanged his pistol, a knife, gunpowder, and a hundred rounds of ammunition for one horse.

young Shoshone woman, Jumping Fish, who was given that name when she leaped into a stream to escape from the same Hidatsa who kidnapped Sacagawea. They cried and talked excitedly. And in the afternoon, as Sacagawea prepared to serve as an interpreter, she suddenly recognized Cameahwait, the Shoshone chief, as her brother. Rushing to him, she threw her arms around him and wept. Just a few weeks earlier Lewis had noted in his journal that Sacagawea never showed emotions. Now, however, in her role as interpreter she paused several times as she broke into tears.

While Sacagawea helped the captains communicate with Cameahwait, the baby Pomp, now six months old, waved his arms in the air from his cradleboard, which was propped nearby. Seaman lay close to Pomp, listening and watching. The giant dog had become the baby's faithful guardian.

The meeting with the Shoshone went well. Cameahwait agreed to trade for horses. He also provided valuable information about the route that the expedition would have to take to reach "the great or stinking lake"—the Pacific Ocean.

➤ August 21–30, 1805

On the afternoon of August 30, the expedition set out again, leaving the Shoshone camp on the Lemhi River with twenty-nine horses in its possession. Most of the horses were to be used as pack animals, with the explorers walking.

Although the Shoshone had driven hard bargains for the horses, the parting was friendly. Lewis was grateful for the help of the Shoshone. On August 25 he went without dinner so some deer meat could be given to Shoshone women and children.

While exploring the Salmon River, Clark briefly described a bird "of the woodpecker kind which fed on Pine burs . . . about the size of a robin." Today the bird bears his name: Clark's nutcracker (top). A few weeks earlier, in present-day Montana, Lewis had described a black woodpecker (bottom) that today is called Lewis's woodpecker. Dozens of other animals and plants first described by Lewis and Clark are not linked to them by name.

A Shoshone guide the captains called Old Toby led the way. He had already proved useful by leading Clark and several men to the valley of the Salmon River. This side trip confirmed Cameahwait's information: the Salmon in that area was impassable by canoe. The expedition would have to reach the Columbia River by heading north, then west over the Bitterroot Mountains.

It was still summer, but this was summer deep in the Rocky Mountains. There were frosts every night, and sometimes a quarter-inch of ice formed on still water. Lewis complained that the ink on his quill pen froze. The Shoshone "inform us we shall shortly have snow," he wrote. The chilly weather was heartily welcomed by Seaman. His thick black hair had made summer heat at times almost unbearable.

⤳ September 3–16, 1805

Summing up September 16, William Clark wrote, "I have been wet and as cold in every part as I ever was in my life, indeed I was at one time fearfull my feet would freeze in the thin mockersons which I wore."

Seaman, and Seaman alone, enjoyed the day because snow began to fall before dawn and continued for hours, covering the ground to a depth of six to eight inches. There had already been several light snowfalls, but this one was perfect for Newfoundland dog play. He buried his head in the fluffy powder.

On September 4 the expedition met a band of Salish Indians (called Flatheads by Lewis and Clark) who were on their way to the western plains to hunt bison with the Shoshone. The friendly and generous Salish exchanged some good horses for a few trade goods.

Seaman's friskiness in the snow was tempered, however, by his hunger. As the expedition struggled through the timber of the Bitterroot Valley and then along Lolo Creek in crossing the Bitterroot Mountains, the hunters found almost no game to kill. The explorers had lost weight. On the 14th they had been forced to kill one of the colts from among their horses. This evening they killed another. Seaman was given very little to eat. He gnawed on bones.

The expedition's journey through this rugged, forested land had been full of mishaps. Precious time had been lost while the men searched for horses that had roamed off in the night, looking for grass to eat. Several packhorses had slipped and tumbled down slopes. Clark's writing desk was smashed, as was the expedition's

On the evening of September 9 the expedition camped where Lolo Creek meets the Bitterroot River. They called the site Traveler's Rest. They hoped to stock up on meat before heading west up the creek and through the Bitterroot Mountains, but the hunters found no game. Old Toby, the Shoshone guide, told Lewis of another river that flowed into the Bitterroot from the east. It led to a low pass over the Continental Divide. If they had known of this route and left the Missouri below the Three Forks, they might have spared themselves seven weeks of upstream struggle.

last thermometer; journal entries noting the temperature came to an end.

❧ September 18, 1805

This morning the last meat of the last colt was eaten for breakfast. The expedition traveled eighteen miles and camped on the side of a steep mountain. For dinner the explorers had a small portion of dried soup that had been carried all the way from Pittsburgh. Lewis had anticipated that they might need it for emergency rations, and this was clearly an emergency as everyone grew weaker each day. Besides soup the only remaining possible food items were bear oil and candles. Killing a horse for food was ruled out because that would mean that some trade goods or other vital baggage would have to be abandoned.

The expedition's main hopes for food rested on Captain Clark, who hurried ahead of the main group with six hunters. They made remarkable progress—thirty-two miles—through a forested landscape littered with many fallen trees. From a mountaintop they saw a vast open plain to the southwest. Still, the men found nothing to hunt. They camped beside a stream that Clark named Hungery Creek because they had no food.

❧ September 21, 1805

Lewis's group made a dinner from a little horse meat, some grouse, a coyote, and crayfish caught in a creek. Lewis wrote, "I find myself growing weak for the want of food and most of the men complain of a similar deficiency."

Help was on the way. Clark had met a band of Nez Perce

people who were gathering camas lily roots from the Weippe Prairie. He loaded a horse with roots and some salmon and ordered Reubin Field to hurry back to Lewis's group with this food.

Many Indian groups from the Pacific Northwest came to the Weippe Prairie to dig out camas roots. Stored and dried, camas could be made into bread and was a key part of their winter diet. There were no bison west of the Rockies, so the Native Americans there ate deer, elk, and great quantities of roots and salmon.

 ## October 7, 1805

At 3 P.M. Seaman settled down on the bottom of a canoe—one of five launched into the North Fork of the Clearwater River. He sensed extraordinary excitement in the voices around him as the canoes were packed and everyone clambered aboard. It was similar to the moment when the expedition left Fort Mandan in the spring—only better. Once again they were setting off into the unknown, but this time they believed they were just a few weeks from their goal—and they were headed *downstream.*

Ever since leaving the Ohio River in mid-November 1803, the men had struggled against the force of flowing water. Now they would have that force pushing them toward the Pacific.

The men left the Nez Perce camp with mixed feelings. On the one hand, they felt friendly toward the Indians and entrusted them with the care of the expedition's horses. A Nez Perce chief, Twisted Hair, had given them

According to the oral history of the Nez Perce, the Indians discussed killing the expedition's advance group—Captain Clark and six hunters—whom they met at Weippe Prairie. They wanted the explorers' modern rifles. But a Nez Perce woman spoke against the plan. She had once been captured by Blackfeet and taken to present-day Canada, where she lived with white traders who treated her well. She urged her people to help, not hurt, the members of the expedition.

directions and drawn a map of the area to the west on an elk-skin. He also showed Clark how to hollow out ponderosa pine logs to make canoes by burning the wood rather than chopping it. Twisted Hair and a lesser chief agreed to come along as interpreters on part of the downstream trip. But in spite of the Nez Perce's help, almost every member of the expedition had bad memories of their visit. They had all fallen ill after reaching the Nez Perce camp at the Weippe Prairie. The change from an all-meat diet to one of roots and salmon had unpleasant results. Just after meeting the Nez Perce on September 20, William Clark wrote, "I find myself verry unwell all the evening from eateing the fish & roots too freely."

On the 27th Clark wrote, "Capt Lewis very Sick nearly all the men Sick." The severe intestinal upset kept many men from working for several days, but some began to recover and help prepare for river travel. Even on the day of departure, both captains felt ill as the canoes were launched downstream.

In the evening of October 9 the Shoshone guide Old Toby fled from the expedition without waiting to be paid and returned to Cameahwait's village. Running the rapids in a canoe apparently terrified him. Today his role in guiding the expedition over the Bitterroot Mountains is recognized as key to its success. The name Old Toby is Lewis and Clark's nickname. The man's Nez Perce name was Swooping Eagle.

Clark continued to record compass directions and estimated miles traveled. The river flowed mostly west, and the canoes passed through nine dangerous rapids. Despite its late start, the Corps of Discovery gained twenty miles this day.

❧ October 10, 1805

For days the canoes had been speeding down the Clearwater, slicing through rapid after rapid, some mild, some wild. Several times a canoe overturned, spilling passengers, baggage, and equipment. At the end of a day damaged canoes had to be repaired and wet trade goods and other items spread out to dry.

Each day the canoes passed several villages of Indians who were part of the Nez Perce nation. Captain Lewis did not take time to stop to speak to the many Indians who watched the canoes speed by. On this day the expedition gained fifty-eight miles and reached the Snake River, even though the group had to stop for an hour in order to free a canoe that had wedged itself on a boulder in the river.

Providing meat for everyone was a problem. Deer and elk lived in the surrounding countryside, but there wasn't much time to hunt. The captains could no longer send men out on day-long hunting expeditions because the canoes moved so swiftly downstream. The Indians were reluctant to part with much of their winter's supply of dried salmon. So the explorers began trading with Indians for another source of meat: dogs.

Unlike Clark, Lewis enjoyed Indian dog meat. Most of the men preferred it to deer or elk. Desperate for meat while proceeding down the Columbia, the expedition traded for scores of dogs. For example, on October 18 it acquired forty in exchange for some bells, thimbles, pins, brass wire, and a few beads. Some of the Pacific Northwest Indians disgustedly called the explorers "dog eaters."

Most of the men had been served dog as a special meal by the Teton Sioux. From this day onward for many weeks it became an important food source for every member of the Corps of Discovery—except one. That one was not Seaman, who eagerly ate cooked dog meat and chewed on dog bones. The one who didn't enjoy it was William Clark. On this day he wrote, "all the Party have greatly the advantage of me, in as much as they all relish the flesh of the dogs, Several of which we purchased."

⇥ October 14, 1805

William Clark had what he called a good dinner "for the first time for three weeks past." He ate ducks called blue-winged teal that had been shot. After the meal the expedition set out again, but the rear canoe hit a rock and turned broadside in a wild rapid. All of the men got out safely before it sank, but some bedding, gunpowder, and dried roots were lost. After battling the current for an hour the men brought the canoe to shore.

Moving swiftly westward, the Corps of Discovery had left a forested landscape and were now passing through a mostly treeless land. There was a new shortage: firewood. This evening the captains allowed the men to break a long-standing rule not to take anything belonging to the Native Americans. Searchers failed to find any wood in any direction, so the expedition used wood that Indians had stored by the river.

⇥ October 17, 1805

The preceding day the canoes had passed from the Snake River into the broader and deeper Columbia River, and now Seaman, sitting behind the bow paddler of a canoe, inhaled a scent that had become stronger and stronger: that of dead fish. The canoes passed by villages where salmon by the thousands were drying in the sun on wooden racks in front of every lodge. Added to odors from these fish was the new smell of dead and decaying salmon. Clark wrote of great numbers of dead salmon on the shores, floating on the water, or lying on the bottom of the river. "the Cause of the emence numbers of dead Salmon I can't account for," he added.

➤ October 20, 1805

Seaman leaped into the river to retrieve four mallard ducks shot by Clark, which became part of dinner. To have a cooking fire, the men often had to collect small dead branches of willows along the river. There was so little firewood that they sometimes had no breakfast.

In his journal, Lewis drew a fish he called the white salmon trout. It is now known as the coho or silver salmon.

Clark and Lewis probably knew about the ways of Atlantic salmon, which differ from salmon of the Pacific Northwest. They were witnessing the end of the fall salmon run, in which males and females mate, leave fertilized eggs, then die without returning to the Pacific.

On this day the canoes traveled forty-two miles. While the goal of the expedition was to get to the ocean as quickly as possible, it still stopped occasionally at villages so that the captains could observe the Indians' clothing and ways of catching salmon as well as the design and construction of their lodges and canoes. At one village Clark saw Indians with red-and-blue cloth robes and one with a sailor's jacket. This clothing could have only come from trading ships that had entered the Columbia River where it joined the Pacific.

→ October 23, 1805

The expedition reached a section of dangerous rapids and falls on the Columbia. The captains studied the first major series of rapids and decided to ride the canoes through some and to lower them by means of elkskin ropes or portage around the worst. All of the equipment and baggage would be carried about a quarter of a mile along the shore. Once underway, one canoe broke free but was caught by Chinook Indians below the rapids.

Clark described great numbers of sea otters below the falls. Hunters shot some, but they sank quickly and could not be recovered. If they had been, the captains would have discovered that the animals were seals. The explorers were still many miles from the Pacific, and Clark corrected the error in February 1806, noting that sea otters lived only along the coast.

Seaman noticed many large animals swimming in the river. He whined, wagged his tail, and looked back at Lewis for permission to go after one. Lewis told him to stay. Both Lewis and Clark called the animals sea otters, but they were actually harbor seals.

→ October 25, 1805

So far the Corps of Discovery had mastered the wildest white water on the Columbia River—"to the astonishment of all the Inds" who gathered to watch from shore, wrote Clark. The men who could not swim carried overland such precious cargo as guns, ammunition, and journals, while the others, and Seaman, rode the canoes through the rapids.

Seaman was included because of his ability to take care of himself in the water and, if necessary, to help rescue anyone who fell in.

The expedition beached the canoes on a gentle stretch of the river below the rapids. There the captains met with the two Nez Perce chiefs for the last time until the following spring. The expedition was now in Chinook country, and the Chinook and the Nez Perce had been at war. After trading for two horses, Twisted Hair and the second Nez Perce chief, Tetoharsky, set out for home. The members of the expedition missed them, especially when they discovered that the Chinook who visited camp were not trustworthy and often tried to steal things.

⤳ October 31–November 2, 1805

On November 2 the explorers cleared the last of the falls and rapids—an area the captains called the Great Shute (later named the Cascades of the Columbia). The river narrowed, and Clark saw "water passing with great velocity forming & boiling in a most horriable manner." They managed to get through.

Below the Great Shute the river widened and looked calm far downstream. When the canoes were beached for the day, Seaman leaped out, eager to stretch his legs and explore the campsite. But first he took a drink. He lapped up some of the river water, then stopped. The water tasted odd.

Most of the rocky wild rapids and falls that the explorers passed through on the Columbia and Snake Rivers exist no more, having been stilled and submerged by a series of dams used to generate electricity. The dams are the main cause of steady declines in salmon populations. Some species of salmon are in danger of extinction. Most fisheries biologists believe that the only way to restore the once-great salmon population is to breach several dams on the Snake River.

91

The men noticed it too, a salty taste. Along the shore they saw other signs that ocean tides now affected the Columbia. They were close to the Pacific!

✤ November 7, 1805

After waiting for a thick fog to clear off, the canoes set out. They passed through thickly wooded countryside as the river widened to more than a mile across. When the fog finally burned off, the explorers could see the river growing even wider and wider. A great expanse of water lay ahead. To the west they heard the sound of waves breaking on a rocky shore.

The men began talking excitedly, then shouting, then cheering. Seaman joined in, barking. William Clark scribbled a quick note: "Ocian in view! O! the joy."

Chapter 4

Winter by the Pacific
and the Journey Home

"**S**CRATCH, SCRATCH, SCRATCH."

"Scratch, scratch, scratch, scratch."

"Scratch, scratch, scratch, scratch, scratch!"

Seaman scratched, and scratched, and scratched some more. Fleas that lived in his thick coat were on the move.

Nearby, some of the men trying to sleep in Fort Clatsop also scratched at fleas. These pesky insects thrived in the damp winter of the Pacific Northwest.

In his journal William Clark reported that Indians sometimes abandoned a village for a time to escape from its fleas. One December night he stayed overnight at a Clatsop village. Soon after laying down on his sleeping mat, he "was attacked most violently by the flees and they kept up a close Siege dureing the night." Even before Fort Clatsop was completely built, Clark wrote, "we find great dificuelty in getting those trouble insects out of our robes and blankets."

Fort Clatsop was the winter home built by the Corps of Discovery. It was a safe but sometimes miserable refuge. Nearly every day was gray and rainy. Food spoiled quickly in the damp climate. The explorers lived mostly on elk, fish, and roots—when they could get them. Trading with the native people for food was limited because the expedition's supply of trade goods was almost gone. (One of the most valuable items for trade, they discovered, was blue beads, but they had few left.)

However, despite the poor food, illness, fleas, boredom, and dreary weather, the explorers felt great pride. They had made it all the way to the Pacific! And in their hearts they kept the bright hope they would start for home in the spring.

On November 7 they had entered the broad estuary of the Columbia River that leads to the ocean. They were still twenty miles from the Pacific coast. Nevertheless, waves almost swamped their canoes. Several men and Sacagawea became seasick. (Seaman did not; many generations of his ancestors had lived aboard sailing ships.) The captains were forced to make camp on a small point of land where, William Clark wrote, there was "scercely room Sufficent for us all to lie Clear of the tide water."

There they were trapped by stormy weather for more than a week. Steep cliffs blocked their way inland, so the men could not hunt. They could scarcely keep a fire lit and were kept busy day and night guarding the canoes from huge dead trees that waves sent crashing into the shore. One day Clark wrote that the wind "blew with violence throwing the water of the river with emence waves out of its banks almost over whelming us in water, O! how horriable is the day."

They survived, thanks to the Clatsop Indians who brought fish and roots to exchange for fishhooks, beads, and other trade goods. The Indians traveled in large canoes that were designed to withstand the wild waves of the Columbia estuary and the Pacific coast. In these craft they safely crossed the five-mile width of the Columbia from their lands on the southern shore of the estuary.

A change in the weather allowed the expedition to retreat upriver from its storm-battered campsite. By late November 1805 the explorers had to choose the site for a winter camp. Should they canoe farther up the river? If they stayed near the ocean, should they build a fort on the north side or the south side of the estuary? Deer were abundant on the north side of the Columbia, but this was the home of Chinook Indians, who at every opportunity tried to steal from the explorers. The Clatsop of the southern shore seemed more honest and reported that both deer and elk were plentiful there. The presence of elk was important. An elk provided more meat than a deer, and elkskin was better than deerskin

The captains probably favored staying near the Pacific, hoping that a trading ship would appear. This would enable the expedition to replenish some supplies. However, they polled everyone's opinion. The votes of York and Sacagawea are considered a remarkable event by some historians, who say that this was the first time in American history that a slave and an Indian woman had voted. More than sixty years would pass before the Civil War ended slavery in the United States, beginning a process that led to voting rights in some states for freed male slaves. In 1890 Wyoming was the first state to allow women to vote. Not until 1920 did women throughout the United States have the right to vote.

for making clothes and moccasins.

On November 24, the captains called everyone together to discuss and vote on the choices. Captain Clark wrote down the name of each person and recorded his or her vote. Both Sacagawea and York had a say. The majority voted to cross the Columbia to see if elk were indeed abundant there and to scout for the site of a winter fort.

Fort Clatsop was built near a river that flowed into the Columbia. The surrounding forest provided plenty of timber for its construction, and fresh water flowed from a nearby spring. Seaman happily lapped up this water. After weeks near the ocean, where the explorers sometimes had to catch rain in containers to drink, everyone was pleased to have a reliable fresh- water spring near the fort.

Fort Clatsop was built about two hundred yards from the river, which today is called the Lewis and Clark River. It measured fifty feet square. Most of the space within its walls was occupied by seven rooms. Clark drew floor plans of the fort in his journal. This made it possible for a replica of the fort to be constructed close to the exact site. Open to visitors, Fort Clatsop National Memorial is near Astoria, Oregon.

Dawn of Christmas day, 1805, was greeted with a volley of gunfire and a song. The Christmas celebration was brief and none too cheerful. Not only were there few gifts to exchange but the day's menu featured only spoiled elk, spoiled fish, and a few roots. The fort's rooms had roofs, but still lacked bunks and chimneys and, of course, it was raining.

Private Joseph Field built desks for the captains, and soon after the fort was complete, on December 30, they were able to begin catching up on journal-writing under a roof. Meriwether Lewis had made almost no entries in his journal for many weeks. On January 1, 1806, he began to write again. Day after day, bent over his candlelit desk in the captains' hut, he wrote about the expedition's many discoveries. He described animals and plants, the lands and waters, the native peoples. He often illustrated his pages with drawings of fish, birds, and Indian canoes.

Outside the hut, birds called and rain dripped from the roof. Inside, Lewis's quill pen scratched on paper while Seaman slept—or scratched at fleas—at his feet.

William Clark also wrote in his journal, often copying Lewis's words in case one journal was lost. He devoted many hours to drawing a map. Working from his compass read-ings; estimates of distances; and notes about rivers, mountains, and other features of the landscape, he showed the expedition's route from Fort Mandan to the Pacific. This map and his map of the route from St. Louis to Fort Mandan combined to make a new and remarkably accurate map of the American West (part of the map is on page 133).

The other members of the Corps of Discovery also spent many productive hours at Fort Clatsop. Despite the wet climate they kept the rifles in good working order—thanks to the metal-working skills of John Shields. From elk hides they made clothes and 358 pairs of moccasins—about 11 per person—which would be needed on the homeward journey of more than four thousand miles.

The men were not fond of sewing and welcomed opportunities to hunt elk or deer. Captain Clark sent one group to the coast to set up a special camp for making salt. The expedition's salt supply had been used up long ago. It was useful for preserving food, and most of the men also craved a salty flavor on their food. Salt was made by pouring seawater into large kettles set over fires. As the water boiled away as vapor, salt crystals were left inside the kettles. By keeping fires blazing under the kettles day and night the men were able to make enough salt to last until they reached a cache of salt they had hidden far to the east, by the Missouri River.

In early January some Clatsop Indians visited the fort to sell some roots, berries, dogs, and a piece of whale blubber. A large whale had been washed ashore about twenty miles from camp. The captains hoped to get more of this bounty of food. On January 5 Clark wrote, "I determine to Set out early tomorrow with two canoes & 12 men in quest of the whale." However, Sacagawea made a strong plea to go, too. She told Clark that she had traveled a long way to see "the great waters," and now that a "monstrous fish" could also be seen, she thought she should be allowed to join the men on this adventure. Clark agreed. With eleven-month-old Pomp in a cradleboard on her back, Sacagawea set out with the others. Seaman remained at the fort with Lewis.

Clark had hoped to travel partway to the whale by canoe, but the group had to walk most of the distance over a steep and slippery route. On January 8 they reached the whale but found only a 105-foot-long skeleton. Nearby, Indians were busy boiling the remaining whale blubber to make oil. Clark was able to trade for some whale oil and blubber, but his hopes of getting a large amount of food from the whale were dashed. Still, everyone was glad they had made the journey. For Sacagawea and most of the men it was a once-in-a-lifetime chance to see the remains of a giant whale.

In late February many of the explorers were ill with bad colds and fevers, perhaps with influenza. Lewis wrote on March 2, 1806, that they recovered slowly because "the diet of the sick is so inferior." Despite the great hunting prowess of George Drouillard, there often wasn't enough to eat—a situation that worsened in early March when the elk of the region began migrating inland.

The captains sped up the preparations for leaving Fort Clatsop. Seaman sensed a change in the moods of the explorers. Although no one looked forward to paddling a canoe upstream again, all were eager to leave their dreary winter home. As they voyaged up the Columbia, through the mountains, and down the Missouri River toward home— there would be horses to ride, bison to eat, and further adventures. In the early afternoon of March 23 they set out in five canoes—thirty-one men, one young woman with her baby, and a Newfoundland dog.

On June 12, 1806, the Lydia, *a trading ship from Boston, sailed into the Columbia estuary. The Indians told the ship's captain of the Lewis and Clark expedition, which had left the area about three months earlier.*

☀ April 10, 1806

Each day, progress up the Columbia grew more difficult as the canoe paddlers struggled against currents that had carried them swiftly downstream the previous fall. On this day they used their single tow rope to advance up the north side of the river.

⤚ April 11, 1806

The men struggled all day, pulling four of the five canoes upstream through powerful rapids. They carried their supplies along a narrow and slippery trail beside the river, whose waters were twelve feet higher than in the autumn. By evening they were too exhausted to haul up the remaining canoe.

All through the day the explorers had to stay alert whenever Indians of the area appeared. Meriwether Lewis wrote, "these are the greates theives and scoundrels we have met with." No tool or item of value could be left unguarded. The explorers sometimes had to threaten the Indians with knives or guns in order to keep them away.

Some members of the local tribe were honest, however. In the evening one of them who spoke the Clatsop language gave Lewis some startling news: his dog had been stolen. Seaman had been lured a half mile away from the expedition, and three Indians were pulling him toward their village.

Clark wrote that an Indian had "decoyed" Seaman nearly half a mile but gave no details about how the dog was lured away. Since the natives of the region did not eat dogs, no one knows whether they meant to harm Seaman.

Lewis ordered three men to pursue the Indians. Their rifles were loaded and ready, and they had their orders: fire on the thieves if they put up the least resistance to surrendering the dog. Fortunately, there was still some light left in the day. Seeing

that they were being chased, the thieves released Seaman and fled. The big dog returned to camp with his rescuers, to the explorers' great relief.

That same evening an Indian was caught stealing an ax, the final act in a day full of attempted thievery. This was the last straw for Meriwether Lewis. Using sign language, he told the Indians gathered near the camp that "if they made any further attempts to steal our property or insulted our men we should put them to instant death." The next day he noted that the Indians "behaved themselves much better."

❧ April 16, 1806

In the evening, Lewis gave Seaman some small dead squirrels to eat. Reubin Field had returned from hunting with two kinds of squirrels. Lewis continued to pursue President Jefferson's goal of learning about the wildlife, plants, and peoples of the unknown West. As usual he examined the squirrels closely, described their colors in his journal, and saved the skins for later scientific study. One species was the western gray squirrel; the others probably belonged to the species now called California ground squirrel.

While the Corps of Discovery explored the American West, the Spanish government grew concerned that the United States would take over its gold and silver mines in the Southwest. One solution, the Spanish thought, would be to find the Lewis and Clark expedition and force it to turn back or take the men prisoner. Over a two-year period, four groups of soldiers set out from Santa Fe and headed north to intercept the expedition. None were successful. However, in the frontier town of St. Louis there were rumors that the explorers had been captured and were being forced to work in the Spanish mines.

For Seaman and all of the others, food was scarce. (Salmon had not yet returned to the river. The Indians survived on roots and dried salmon from the previous year.) The expedition's hunters ranged as far as possible in search of deer, while Lewis and Clark traded with the Indians for roots, dried fish, and dogs.

Sometimes they had to trade for another basic need: firewood. They had left the lush forests of the lower Columbia and were surrounded by vast grassy plains. Wood was so scarce that the expedition sometimes had just one fire for cooking and warmth during the cold nights.

❧ April 18, 1806

The men cut up two canoes for firewood, and the captains traded elkskins and a few other items for several horses. They had concluded that pulling canoes upstream through the rapids of the Columbia was an unnecessary ordeal. They would eventually carry all of the expedition's baggage on packhorses.

⋙ April 24, 1806

On the preceding day an Indian had offered a horse in exchange for one of the remaining canoes. He withdrew his offer when he realized that the expedition was about to begin travel by land and that the canoes would be abandoned. Annoyed at the loss of a needed horse, Lewis decided to cut the canoes into firewood. He told George Drouillard to begin. One swing of his tomahawk knocked off a chunk of wood, and the Indian quickly offered several strands of beads for the canoes. Lewis accepted the trade. The beads would soon be useful in trades for dogs or other food.

⋙ April 28, 1806

Seaman lay beside Meriwether Lewis, gazing with great interest at the spectacle before them: more than five hundred men, women, and children of the Yakima and Wallawalla tribes dancing by the light of the campfires. Earlier in the evening Pierre Cruzatte had played his fiddle, and some of the explorers had danced for the Indians.

The captains were able to communicate well with the Wallawalla, using Sacagawea as an interpreter. A Shoshone woman was being held prisoner by the Wallawalla, so Sacagawea was able to ask and answer many questions in the language they both knew.

By now the expedition had been able to trade for twenty-three horses. They soon started eastward again, taking a shortcut the Wallawalla recommended that spared them eighty miles of walking. In their journals the captains had nothing but praise for the Wallawalla—"the most hospitable, honest, and sincere people that we have met with in our voyage"—in contrast to some of the Indians they had encountered along the Columbia.

≫ May 7, 1806

The men caught sight of mountains to the east. They were the Bitterroots, "perfectly Covered with Snow," Lewis wrote, through which the expedition would have to pass. The captains were discouraged by information from the Nez Perce, whose territory the expedition had reached. Unusually heavy snows had fallen that winter, the Nez Perce told them. No one could pass through the mountains until after the next full moon—early June or later.

This was bad news, particularly because food was so scarce. The Nez Perce had little to spare, and the explorers had few items to use in trade. However, the Nez Perce would trade horses, dogs, and dried roots for medical services. They came to William Clark with a variety of ailments. He cleaned and dressed wounds and applied ointments. Both Clark and

Lewis doubted that their medicines did much good, but the Nez Perce were eager for this doctoring. The preceding day a Nez Perce man had given Clark a young horse in payment for Clark's treating an abscess on his wife's back. The horse was immediately killed to provide dinner for the explorers.

⟫ May 8, 1806

Several hunters set out at first light and shot three deer. Another deer, though wounded, might have escaped, but Seaman chased and caught it a little distance from camp. The expedition had enough food for the day.

⟫ May 14–17, 1806

The expedition made camp by a river in Nez Perce territory. Not far away were timber for firewood and fine grass for the horses. The men also found small wild onions growing in the meadows, and Sacagewea dug up roots—"very agreeable food"— that tasted like annis seed. Here the expedition would wait until more snow melted in the mountains that loomed ahead. Lewis

The Corps of Discovery stayed at Camp Chopunnish, as it came to be called, for nearly a month. It was located near present-day Kamiah, Idaho, on the eastern side of the Clearwater River near the eastern boundary of the Nez Perce reservation.

wrote, "as we are compelled to reside a while in this neighbourhood I feel perfectly satisfyed with our position."

All welcomed the possibility that salmon might soon be swimming upstream. Seaman and the others began to have a little more variety in their diets, as the hunters shot some grizzly and black bears. The captains were worried about the ferocious grizzlies and ordered the hunters to travel in pairs for protection. On this day some of the bear meat was shared with fifteen Nez Perce who were visiting.

❧ May 22, 1806

Seaman gave a worried whine and licked the face of Pomp, who had been sick for several days. Sacagawea's child was now fifteen months old. He was cutting teeth and had been fussy, but something more serious was troubling him—a swollen throat and a high fever. The captains did their best doctoring: "we gave him a doze of creem of tartar and flour of sulpher and applyed a poltice of boiled onions to his neck as warm as he could well bear it."

Physicians have tried to figure out the cause of Pomp's symptoms. One possibility is mumps, another is tonsillitis. About two weeks passed before he recovered fully.

❧ May 23, 1806

Early this morning Nathaniel Pryor wounded a deer near camp. Seaman chased it. The deer leaped into the river and crossed to the opposite shore. Two young Nez Perce men mounted their horses, swam across the river, and drove the deer back toward camp, where Pryor killed it. The meat was shared with the Indians.

Lewis and Clark continued to apply medicines, including onion poultices, to little Pomp, and his fever lessened.

❧ May 31, 1806

The Nez Perce brought to camp the last of the horses they had agreed to keep for the winter. From this supply and from various trades, the expedition now had a herd of sixty-five horses. Most were in good condition. The explorers were eager to get underway. The captains looked often at the distant mountains, noting that the snow had melted from some lower slopes. They paid close attention to the level of the river by the camp. The more it rose, they reasoned, the more snow had melted in the mountains. Between sunset this day and dawn on June 1 the river rose eighteen inches.

❯❯ June 2, 1806

Feeding more than thirty people every day continued to be a challenge. In desperation, this morning the captains sent Hugh McNeal and York to a Nez Perce village with some new trade items: the brass buttons from the coats of their military uniforms. The men returned with some bread and three bushels of roots.

❯❯ June 9, 1806

"we eat the last of our meat yesterday evening and have lived on roots today," wrote Meriwether Lewis. Despite the lack of food, the group was cheerful, "much elated with the idea of moving on towards their friends and country."

While waiting for the snow to melt in the mountains, the men sometimes enjoyed competing with the Nez Perce in footraces, horseraces, and shooting. In horseback riding and in accuracy with bow and arrow, the explorers were no match for the Indians.

❯❯ June 10, 1806

Seaman trotted alongside Meriwether Lewis's horse as the Corps of Discovery set out eastward into the mountains.

All the explorers were on horseback, with many extra horses carrying baggage. The expedition got underway despite the advice of the Nez Perce, who warned that the extraordinary snows of the past winter might not allow passage through the Rockies until early July.

⤝ June 17, 1806

After pausing for a few days at the Weippe Prairie, where the preceding September the explorers had eaten many lily roots to stave off starvation, the expedition set out again. The explorers had no guides and hoped that the snow had melted so that the trail through the mountains would be visible. They struggled around and over rocks and fallen trees on a slippery trail in the valley of Hungery Creek (so named by Clark last September).

Then travel became easier. Deep snow covered the obstacles on the trail. Lewis wrote, "we found ourselves invelloped in snow from 12 to 15 feet deep even on the south sides of the hills with the fairest exposure to the sun; here was winter with all it's rigors; the air was cold, my hands and feet were benumbed."

The snow's frozen surface was firm enough that Seaman and even the horses could walk on it without breaking through. But the trail through the mountains was now hidden. And the warnings of the Nez Perce proved correct: there was no grass for the horses to eat. Lewis and Clark recognized that it would be foolish to continue—many horses might die, and the expedition might become lost. After storing supplies and baggage that would not be needed for a while, the explorers turned back. They were dejected. For the first time in the entire journey they had had to retreat.

❧ June 25, 1806

Lewis's feelings of frustration had been growing for several days. On June 18 he had assigned two men to travel to the Nez Perce village to hire guides, but they had not returned. At last, on the afternoon of June 23 the men had rejoined the expedition, bringing three young Nez Perce men. (Two Nez Perce teenagers also joined them.) The expedition set out toward the mountains at first light the next morning.

At midmorning on the 25th the explorers reached the cache of supplies they had left nine days earlier. While quite a bit of snow had melted, it was still several feet deep. The explorers traveled as fast as possible, urged on by their Nez Perce guides. Late this evening they reached the south side of a mountain where the snow had all melted. "Here we found an abundance of fine grass for our horses," Lewis wrote.

❧ June 27–29, 1806

In their journals both Lewis and Clark praised their Nez Perce guides. "These fellows are most admireable pilots," Lewis wrote. They had led the expedition through the still-snowy Bitterroot Mountains and on every day but one found places where the horses had grass to eat.

On June 29 the explorers made camp near warm springs that flowed from the base of a hill. The water in some of the springs was too hot to touch for more than a few seconds. Other

The expedition had also visited the hot springs on their way west, on September 13, 1805, but had not bathed in them. In recent years the temperature of the springs is about 111 degrees Fahrenheit. Lolo Hot Springs is located in western Montana, just east of the Idaho border.

springs were cooler, and the Nez Perce and many of the explorers bathed in them. Meriwether Lewis stayed in one for as long as he could stand the heat—nineteen minutes. Seaman was ready to plunge in beside his master but sensed the heat rising from the water and turned away. Usually he loved to be in water, but not this strange, hot stuff.

⇒ July 3–4, 1806

As the expedition descended the eastern side of the Bitterroots, they passed from an early spring climate to one of early summer. The nights were still cold, but the daytime air was warm—and often full of mosquitoes. Lewis ordered large fires to be built so that the smoke would give the horses some protection from the "excessively troublesome" mosquitoes.

They reached the campsite called Traveler's Rest, where they had stayed for a few days the preceding September. Now the Nez Perce guides wanted to go back to their home west of the Rockies. They worried about meeting a war party of their enemies, the Hidatsa. Before parting they gave the captains further advice on the best route to follow eastward, and Lewis made sure they had a good supply of deer meat. Both the Nez Perce and the explorers felt regret at saying good-bye.

The third of July marked another parting: the Corps of Discovery split into two groups in order to explore rivers that flowed into the Missouri. The captains discussed this possibility at Fort Clatsop, and now Lewis and Clark

By splitting the group, the expedition could gain important information about the best possible overland route from the upper Missouri through the Rockies, plus other details about the uncharted West. However, the smaller groups, though well-armed, would be more vulnerable to attack by hostile Indians.

each set out on different missions. Their plans called for the two groups to divide even more. If all went well, the explorers would meet in five or six weeks where the Yellowstone River joined the Missouri. To accomplish this, Meriwether Lewis would travel nearly eight hundred miles, William Clark almost a thousand.

With twenty men and most of the horses, plus Sacagawea and Pomp, Clark started south on July 3. Riding alongside the Bitterroot River, heading upstream, the group traveled thirty-six miles the first day.

⇥ July 5, 1806

Lewis traveled east northeast with his dog, nine men, and seventeen horses, riding parallel to a river that the Nez Perce called River of the Road to Buffalo (now called the Clark Fork River). They covered thirty-one miles. In the evening, shortly before making camp, they crossed a creek twenty yards wide that flowed into the river. Lewis decided that it was long past time to honor his faithful dog, so he named the stream Seaman's Creek.

Seaman's Creek flows into the Blackfoot River a few miles west of Ovando, Montana. Since Lewis's journals were not published for many years, few people knew of his intention to name it for his dog. So the stream was named Monture Creek in the late 1800s, after a man who was killed in the area by Indians.

⇥ July 7, 1806

In brief notes about this day, Lewis wrote that Reubin Field had wounded a moose near camp in the morning. Then he added, "my dog much worried." Seaman was accustomed to helping hunters kill deer and pronghorns, but a huge moose was much more of a challenge.

Later in the day they traveled though a low mountain pass that Lewis recognized as "the dividing ridge betwen the waters of the Columbia and Missouri rivers"—the Continental Divide. They had left the Oregon Territory and were now back in the territory of the United States. Seaman inhaled a scent that he remembered from the previous September: bison. Lewis noted in his journal the finding of old bison tracks and dung.

❧ July 11, 1806

Lewis's group reached the Missouri River at the White Bear Islands, where the expedition had hidden supplies in mid-July 1805 after struggling past the Great Falls. After months of frequent uncertainty about their next meal, the explorers found themselves overwhelmed with nature's bounty. On the preceding day they had "killed five deer 3 Elk and a bear." They also found red gooseberries beginning to ripen.

Lewis wrote, "I sincerely belief that there were not less than 10 thousand buffaloe within a circle of 2 miles arround that place." They killed eleven bison—for food but also for the hides, which they attached to a framework of willow sticks to make round boats (called bull boats) that they needed to cross the river. (The men had seen the Mandan use such boats.)

Seaman slept very little. He was on guard. The explorers saw wolves every day and heard them every night. The wolves' howls were nearly drowned out by the bellows of bison bulls. Lewis wrote, "there are such numbers of them that there is one continual roar." The expedition's horses were nervous. Born and raised west of the Rockies, they had never seen bison or heard the bulls in mating season.

❯❯ July 15, 1806

At times during the past two years it had seemed that the Lewis and Clark expedition was leading a charmed life. Beginning on July 12, however, a chain of events suggested that its luck had finally run out. On that morning, ten of the seventeen horses were missing, probably stolen by Indians. Lewis sent Joseph Field and George Drouillard in search of them. In the meantime, Lewis and the others crossed to the eastern shore of the Missouri with the remaining horses and made camp. At darkness only Field returned, with no horses.

On the 13th Lewis opened the cache of supplies and other items hidden near the Missouri in 1805. The river had risen higher than expected, and he found that the medicines and many other things were ruined. The greatest loss was the many specimens of plants that Lewis had carefully dried and labeled, which he had planned to take to President Jefferson and to botanists back East.

By noon on July 15 Drouillard had still not returned. Lewis decided that he had probably been killed by a grizzly. He planned to launch a search for the invaluable Drouillard the next morning. Then, at 1 P.M., Drouillard rode into camp. After much searching he had found the abandoned campsite of the Indians who had taken the horses, but it was then too late to pursue them.

The explorers were jubilant at George Drouillard's safe return. But on the same day another member of Lewis's group was almost killed. Hugh McNeal's horse, frightened by a grizzly, threw him off right in front of the bear. McNeal managed to escape by hitting the bear on the head with his gun and then scrambling up a willow tree. The grizzly waited beneath the tree for several hours before finally leaving. McNeal returned safely to camp a little before dark.

Meriwether Lewis wrote about this eventful day beneath his mosquito netting, where he spent as much time as possible. His last few sentences were about mosquitoes. "my dog even howls with the torture he experiences from them . . . they are so numerous that we frequently get them in our thrats as we breath."

Lewis's words about mosquitoes mark the last mention of Seaman in the expedition's journals. Any mention of the dog from this date on is speculation by the author, based on evidence—described in the Afterword—that Seaman probably did return safely.

⇒ July 22, 1806

The loss of the horses caused Meriwether Lewis to change his plans for exploring the Marias River. He had set out on July 16 with three men rather than six. The rest of the men, and Seaman, had stayed at the Missouri. Their job was to haul canoes and baggage around the Great Falls. They would be helped by Sergeant John Ordway, who had started out as part of William Clark's group. He and nine men were traveling down the Missouri in canoes that the expedition had hidden when it obtained horses from the Shoshone. According to the plan, the combined group of thirteen men would canoe down the river until they reached the mouth of the Marias River. If all went well, they would meet Captain Lewis and the other three men there.

In his journal Lewis expressed increased worry about meeting the Indians of the region. The Mandan, Shoshone, and Nez Perce had all warned about the Blackfeet, whom Lewis described as "vicious lawless." He was accompanied only by Drouillard and Joseph and Reubin Field, and he knew that the four of them might be badly outnumbered if they encountered Indians. Lewis never wrote about being killed, but he expected that they might be robbed of horses and weapons. He and his group were especially alert as they explored up the Marias. Lewis scanned the countryside with a telescope.

As he had for many months, Meriwether Lewis wrote in his journal about the landscape, plants, and wildlife. (He also mentioned the temperature—so hot on the 20th that they simply stopped riding for four hours.) His goal now was to see how far north the Marias River extended. Since it drained into the Missouri, the northernmost reach of the Marias could be considered U.S. territory. As the days passed, the river's course—and then that of its tributary, Cut Bank Creek—turned more to the west than the north. On July 22, the men were within ten miles of the Rocky Mountains, and Lewis concluded that the river would not run any farther north.

He felt it was important to make observations that would allow the latitude and longitude of the place to be calculated later. To accomplish this, clear skies were needed. This evening the sky was cloudy. Lewis hoped that the next day would be clear. He was anxious to get back to the Missouri. His men had found plenty of signs near their camp that Indians hunted in the area.

✦ July 24, 1806

While Meriwether Lewis waited for the final step in achieving his goal, William Clark was making good progress in his exploration of the Yellowstone River. In his journal he praised Sacagawea, who recognized landmarks from her childhood and on July 6 pointed out the route they should take. Two days later they reached their camp of the preceding August 17, a place they had named Camp Fortunate. They retrieved the canoes they had sunk in the Beaverhead River near its junction with the Jefferson River. They also dug up some buried supplies, including tobacco. The men who smoked or chewed tobacco were delighted, having gone without for many months.

Clark's group traveled northeast down the Jefferson River, some in canoes and some on horseback. Each day they recognized landmarks and campsites from the previous August. They found plenty of game to kill for food and—as the weather warmed—plenty of mosquitoes.

At noon on July 13, the waters of the Jefferson River had carried Clark's canoes to the Three Forks, where they joined the Madison and Gallatin Rivers. Sergeant Pryor and his men had arrived an hour earlier with the horses. The men had spent a busy afternoon, following Clark's orders, as they prepared to split up. After an early dinner, Sergeant Ordway had set out in six canoes with nine men, heading down the Missouri to meet with Captain Lewis's group at the Great Falls.

Clark had been left with ten men, Sacagawea and Pomp, and forty-nine horses and a colt. Once again, Sacagawea was a helpful guide. She remembered the area and recommended taking a certain gap through the mountains, the best pass to use to reach the Yellowstone River. Once at the Yellowstone, two days later, they began searching for trees large enough to make into canoes. Finding none, they rode their horses downstream along the river.

Not until July 20 did they cut down two cottonwood trees big enough to be hollowed out and shaped into canoes—a project that was not completed until noon on the 23rd. Meanwhile, there had been alarming news on the morning of July 21: half of their horses were missing, probably stolen by Crow Indians. Clark's men wouldn't even find their tracks to follow until another two days had passed.

Clark's group was especially eager to make at least one canoe because one man, George Gibson, fell from his horse onto a sharp stub of a tree limb, driving it two inches into his thigh. This painful wound made it difficult for Gibson to travel by horse. On July 19, John Shields was sent scouting on horseback for a tree big enough to make into a canoe. He found none and was chased by two grizzly bears.

The loss of the horses was disappointing, since Lewis and Clark had planned to give all of the expedition's horses to the Mandan, hundreds of miles to the east. Now this gift was half of its intended size. Nevertheless, on July 24, Sergeant Nathaniel Pryor and three men set out overland with the horses.

After noting the incredible numbers of buffalo, elk, and pronghorn antelope—"we have a great abundance of the best of meat"—Clark and the remainder of his group launched the new canoes downstream. Helped by the Yellowstone's rapid current, they made sixty-nine miles that day.

❧ July 26, 1806

"we set out biding a lasting adieu to this place which I now call camp disappointment," Lewis wrote. The sky had

117

not cleared, so he was unable to observe the sun or stars to help establish the campsite's exact location. The four men headed southeast from Camp Disappointment, aiming for the Missouri River. Lewis paused to take notes about the landscape, plants, and a small species of fox, the swift fox. Riding to the top of a hill, he scanned the land ahead with his telescope and saw "a very unpleasant sight": about thirty horses and several Indians.

Lewis knew that his group had no chance of outrunning the Indians, so he decided to approach them in a friendly manner. From their clothing he suspected that they were Blackfeet, and he was relieved to see that there were only eight of them. The two groups met cautiously, shook hands, and tried to communicate with sign language. Lewis gave some gifts and proposed that they all camp together for the night.

That evening, with Drouillard serving as interpreter, Lewis had "much conversation" with the Blackfeet, learning that they were part of a large group camped a half-day's ride away. Even more Blackfeet were hunting buffalo on the plains and would be heading to the mouth of the Marias River. Lewis told the Indians about the expedition's journey and of President Jefferson's desire for trade with the western natives and for an end to war among the tribes. He proposed that Blackfeet chiefs come to the mouth of the Marias River for a meeting.

As everyone settled down for the night, Lewis took the first watch, until 11:30 P.M. Reubin Field took his place, with the trusty Drouillard to follow.

❧ July 27, 1806

Joseph Field was on guard as dawn broke. The eight Blackfeet arose and gathered around the campfire. Field carelessly stepped away from his rifle, which lay near that of his sleeping brother. Suddenly, one Indian grabbed both rifles and began running away. Two other Blackfeet seized the guns of the sleeping Lewis and Drouillard.

Joseph Field yelled. His brother Reubin leaped up, and they both ran after the man who had taken their guns. Reubin Field caught up with the thief, drew his knife, and stabbed him in the heart as they wrestled for the rifles.

Lewis later wrote, "I jumped up and asked what was the matter which I quickly learned when I saw drewyer in a scuffle with the indian for his gun. I reached to seize my gun but found her gone, I then drew a pistol from my holster and terning myself about saw the indian making off with my gun."

Lewis caught up with the thief and motioned for him to lay the rifle on the ground. This he did, perhaps because he saw the Field brothers racing toward them with their recovered rifles and Lewis had his pistol drawn. Drouillard had fought successfully for his rifle, and all three men asked Lewis for permission to shoot the thieves. Lewis said no. Then he saw that the remaining Blackfeet were trying to drive off all the horses.

While his three men raced to catch up with the main group of horses, Lewis pursued two Blackfeet who were herding others, including Lewis's own, into an opening in the steep wall of a bluff. One Blackfeet hid behind a boulder. Lewis raised his rifle, shouting that he would shoot

Historians disagree about the exact location of the fight with the Blackfeet—the expedition's northernmost campsite on the Great Plains. It is about fourteen miles southwest of the town of Cut Bank, Montana, near the Two Medicine River on the Blackfeet Reservation. The Blackfeet man who fired at Lewis probably used an old musket that was less accurate than the rifles used by the Corps of Discovery.

if his horse wasn't returned. The other man, just thirty paces away, turned toward Lewis with a gun. Lewis fired, wounding him. The man fell, then fired his musket at Lewis, who later wrote, "he overshot me . . . I felt the wind of his bullet very distinctly."

Lewis didn't have gunpowder to reload, so he returned to camp. The Field brothers had recovered some of their horses as well as other horses belonging to the Blackfeet that had been left near camp. The explorers quickly caught and saddled the best mounts and packed their belongings. Lewis knew they had to hurry. After nearly two years of peaceful encounters with more than a dozen Native American tribes, including the hostile Teton Sioux and the thieving Chinook, violence had erupted, blood had been shed.

They had killed one and possibly two Blackfeet. They were deep in Blackfeet country. Scores of warriors might soon be hot on their trail. Moreover, Lewis had told the Blackfeet where he was headed, to the place where the Marias River joined the Missouri. The Blackfeet might cut him off or attack the men canoeing down the Missouri. Lewis wrote, "no time was therefore to be lost and we pushed our horses as hard as they would bear."

By midafternoon they had ridden more than sixty miles. After a rest they rode seventeen miles farther. After dark they traveled by moonlight, at a slower pace, passing huge herds of bison. They gained another twenty miles before exhaustion forced them to stop at 2 A.M.

⤜ July 28, 1806

The explorers were so sore from riding that they could hardly stand. Nevertheless, Lewis ordered the men to mount up and continue their race to the Missouri. He also outlined a plan of defense in case they were attacked on the plains by the Blackfeet.

Lewis and his men reached the Missouri, then rode parallel to it downstream for several miles. Suddenly they heard gunfire—the distinctive sound of the modern rifles used by the Corps of Discovery. They rode fast toward the sound, "and on arriving at the bank of the river had the unspeakable satisfaction to see our canoes coming down."

They rode down the bluff to greet the men in the canoes. Hearing Lewis's voice, Seaman began to bark. His tail wagged as fast as a Newfoundland's tail can wag.

After a hasty but joyful reunion on the bank of the Missouri, Lewis's group released their horses and joined the others in the canoes. Hurrying downriver they landed twice to uncover supplies they had hidden in 1805. Near the mouth of the Marias River they found the red pirogue, but its wood was decayed beyond repair. They proceeded on in the white pirogue and five canoes. When they finally made camp on the southwest shore, the wide Missouri River was between the explorers and the Blackfeet. Though some men took turns standing guard in the night, the day that had begun with fear and anxiety probably ended in feelings of safety and triumph.

✺ August 4, 1806

Unaware of Meriwether Lewis's almost disastrous trip up the Marias River, William Clark's group had made good progress down the Yellowstone. On July 25 Clark paused to explore "a remarkable rock," two hundred feet high, and wrote details about the landscape he could see from its top. Finding some Indian carvings in the rock's face, he probably used his knife to mark the sandstone himself: "Wm Clark July 25 1806." He named the rock Pompys Tower, in honor of Sacagawea's son, now nearly eighteen months old.

The two canoes made swift progress—eighty miles on July 27, seventy-three on the 28th. In his journal, Clark described

the passing landscape, reported on wildlife and what the hunters brought in for food, and casually noted other events: "was near being bit by a rattle Snake." On August 2 the canoes halted as a huge herd of bison crossed the river. The men then paddled quickly downstream to avoid another herd that was about to cross. The plentiful bison

The landmark that Clark called Pompys Tower is now called Pompeys Pillar. It is northeast of Billings, Montana. Clark's carving in the sandstone has been protected and is still visible. The Yellowstone River joins the Missouri in North Dakota, just east of the Montana border.

attracted grizzly bears, and Clark's group had almost daily encounters with the dangerous grizzlies.

These days Clark wrote more about mosquitoes than bears. On the morning of August 3 he wrote, "last night the

Musquetors was so troublesom that no one of the party Slept half the night. for my part I did not Sleep one hour." There was little relief from mosquitoes when the canoes reached the Missouri later that day. All of the mosquito netting and blankets had holes. Clouds of the insects surrounded the men when they went hunting and when they tried to make clothing from animal hides. Pomp's face was swollen from many mosquito bites.

The only relief came when they camped on sandbars in the Missouri or when the wind blew. Clark decided to head downriver in hopes of finding fewer mosquitoes there. He wrote of his plan in a note to Lewis, which he tied to a pole stuck into the bank at a prominent bend in the river before fleeing downstream.

❧ August 7, 1806

Captain Lewis, Seaman, and fourteen men sped down the Missouri, eager to reach the Yellowstone and rejoin William Clark. (They were troubled by mosquitoes, too, though Lewis's journal contains fewer complaints than Clark's.) On August 6 they were delayed by a violent wind and rainstorm. On the 7th Lewis wrote, "we set out early resolving if possible to reach the Yelowstone river today which was at the distance of 83 ms. from our encampment of the last evening: the currant favoured our progress being more rapid than yesterday, the men plyed their oars faithfully and we went at a good rate."

Seaman rested in the pirogue, watching the wildlife along the shore and inhaling its scent: bison, elk, deer, and grizzly bears. The hunters had no trouble getting enough meat for all.

At 4 P.M. the boats reached the point near the mouth

of the Yellowstone where Clark had camped. Lewis found part of the note that Clark had left just three days before. He ordered the boats launched again in hopes of catching up with Clark's group at its evening campsite but gave up when darkness fell.

⇸ August 8, 1806

Clark was camped many miles downstream. At 8 A.M. one of the men shouted. There were boats coming down the river! Everyone rushed to the shore, expecting to see Meriwether Lewis and his group in canoes. Instead they saw a puzzling sight: four men in two bull boats.

It was Sergeant Pryor and the three men who were last seen on July 24, far up the Yellowstone. Their mission had been to deliver the expedition's remaining horses to the Mandan, but the entire herd was stolen on the second night of their journey. They had set out on foot for the Yellowstone, where they shot two bison and made boats from their skin. The bull boats had carried them safely for hundreds of miles to rejoin the expedition.

⇸ August 11, 1806

Lewis wondered why he had not yet caught up with Clark. However, rather than racing down the river in pursuit, he decided to pause at times to repair the boats and to allow time for the men to make new clothes from skins of elk, deer, and bison.

At about noon the men in the lead canoes saw a herd of elk in a thicket of willow trees on a sandbar. Leaving his dog on the pirogue, Lewis chose Pierre Cruzatte to join him in hunting elk. Lewis quickly shot one. Cruzatte wounded another. They reloaded their rifles and took different routes through the thick willows.

Lewis saw an elk and raised his rifle to aim. Crack! A rifle fired, and Lewis was shot! A rifle ball passed through his left buttock and left a gash on his right one. "I instantly supposed that Cruzatte had shot me in mistake for an Elk as I was dressed in brown leather and he cannot see very well."

Lewis called out, "damn you, you have shot me," but Cruzatte did not answer. Lewis yelled Cruzatte's name several times. No reply. He began to suspect an Indian attack. After calling for Cruzatte to retreat, Lewis hurried back to the boats and ordered all the men to arm themselves and advance into the willows to look for Cruzatte. He returned to the pirogue; his wound was too painful to allow him to walk. After twenty anxious minutes, he was relieved to see all the men return, bringing Cruzatte with them. They hadn't seen any Indians. Cruzatte insisted that he had shot at an elk and that he had not heard Lewis calling his name. Lewis dropped the matter.

Since Cruzatte was blind in one eye and nearsighted in the other, he was not the best choice of hunting partner in a willow thicket! The rifle ball that wounded Lewis was found in his pants. It came from the kind of U.S. Army rifle the explorers carried. No western Indians had such rifles, so Lewis had no doubt about who had fired the shot. Cruzatte might have been punished early in the expedition, but not now. He had proved his worth countless times with hard work, his fiddle-playing, and his skill with boats.

With the help of Patrick Gass, Lewis washed and dressed his wound. Lewis wrote about the rifle ball: "I was hapy to find that it had touched neither bone nor artery." He was in great pain, though, and moved as little as possible. He spent a feverish night aboard the pirogue with Seaman sleeping close by his side.

❧ August 12, 1806

Seaman kept close to his wounded master until 1 P.M., when the pirogue and canoes rounded a bend in the Missouri and came upon Clark's group, still at its overnight campsite. The two groups shouted back and forth, then talked excitedly as the boats landed. There were so many adventures to share. Seaman leaped ashore, where he was hailed or patted by the men in Clark's group. Wagging his tail, he headed straight for Sacagawea and Pomp, who toddled up to the big dog and buried his arms in his thick fur.

William Clark's joy at seeing Lewis's boats was quickly tempered by the news of his partner's wound. He rushed to the pirogue and was relieved to find Meriwether conscious. Lewis reassured Clark that his wound, though painful, would heal in a month or less.

With the Corps of Discovery completely reunited, the explorers prepared to head down the Missouri toward St. Louis as quickly as possible. Meriwether Lewis knew he would begin this last journey lying on his stomach in the pirogue. It was painful for him to write, so he scrawled, "I shall desist untill I recover and leave to my frind Capt. C. the continuation of our journal."

However, being Meriwether Lewis, he also made a final observation about nature. He had noticed an unfamiliar kind of cherry tree and asked that some of its leaves and fruit be brought to him. Using his knowledge of botany, Lewis described the pin cherry tree in fine detail, including the taste of its fruit. He then wrote the last sentence in his journal: "I have never seen it in blume."

❧ August 14–17, 1806

The explorers had been warmly greeted by the Mandan, whose village they had reached on August 14. Seaman was curious, as usual, about the dogs of the Mandan villages but stayed with Lewis, who still couldn't walk. Clark renewed his friendship with the chiefs, especially Black Cat and Big White. He invited them to accompany the expedition east so that they could meet "their great father," President Jefferson, but the chiefs were worried about passing through the territory of the Teton

Sioux. A Sioux raiding party had recently killed several Mandan.

Big White finally agreed to accompany Lewis and Clark as long as he could bring five others, including his wife and son. There was enough room in the canoes for the Mandan be- cause others were leaving the expedition. John Colter had asked permission to leave the Corps of Discovery. He wanted to join fur trappers who aimed to head up the Missouri. Clark and Lewis agreed and gave Colter gunpowder and other supplies.

Although Toussaint Charbonneau wanted to continue as interpreter for the expedition, his services were no longer needed. Clark invited him to stay with the group as far as St. Louis, but Charbonneau felt he had few job prospects there and decided to stay with the Mandan. Clark paid him for his services, as he had Colter. He also made an extraordinary offer to Charbonneau and Sacagawea: to take Jean Baptiste "Pomp" Charbonneau, then eighteen months old, home with him to raise and educate. They declined because Pomp was still nursing. Clark wrote, "they observed that in one year the boy would be Sufficiently old to leave his mother & he would then take him to me if I would be so freindly as to raise the Child for him in Such a manner as I thought proper, to which I agreeed."

On August 20, William Clark wrote to Charbonneau, expressing regret that Sacagawea could not be paid or rewarded in any way for her help on "that long dangerous and fatigueing rout to the Pacific Ocian and back."

August 17, 1806, was marked by many fond farewells and many tears. The women of Big White's village wailed as he and his family members walked to the canoes that would carry them far, far away. John Colter shook hands with the captains and the other men, with whom he had shared so many hardships and adventures. Then he bent down and shook Seaman's paw. Sacagawea made sure that her son said good-bye to his dog friend, too.

❧ August 27, 1806

The preceding day the expedition gained sixty miles, passing the place where the Teton Sioux had tried to stop the expedition in September 1804. There were no recent signs that the Sioux were nearby, but Clark wrote, "we were much on our guard deturmined to put up with no insults from those bands of Seioux."

On this day the expedition traveled just forty-five miles. The supply of meat was exhausted, so the boats paused more than once while hunters went after elk and bison. Four buffalo and one elk were killed. While waiting with the boats, Meriwether Lewis decided to take a long walk on a sandbar. Seaman stayed very close to his wounded master these days and was delighted to be on the move with him again. But Lewis had not recovered from his wound as much as he had hoped, and Clark wrote that he was "very unwell all night."

❧ September 2, 1806

This evening the explorers camped on a sandbar to escape the still-troublesome mosquitoes. In his journal Clark often remarked how the Missouri River had rearranged itself since they traveled upstream in 1804. Channels, sandbars, and islands had grown larger, shifted position, or disappeared entirely.

In the evening hunters brought in two wild turkeys—creatures that Seaman had not smelled in two years—and a kind of bird that was entirely new to Big White and the other Mandan and that they "very much admired."

⇒ September 4, 1806

At midday the captains ordered the boats to halt at Sergeant Floyds Bluff. The men climbed the hill to visit the grave of Charles Floyd—remarkably, the only man of the Corps to die during the entire expedition.

⇒ September 6, 1806

Almost every day the Corps of Discovery met fur trappers and traders heading upstream. On this day the captains bought a gallon of whiskey from a trader and gave each of their men a dram. It was their first taste of liquor since the Fourth of July, 1805.

Meriwether Lewis was especially interested in election results and was pleased to learn that Jefferson had won reelection as president.

The explorers had no idea of events taking place in the United States for the past twenty-eight months and were eager for news. They soon discovered that they themselves were news: nearly everyone had given them up for dead a year ago!

⇒ September 18, 1806

In William Clark's journal he sometimes complained of the pace—"we only decended 49 miles today," he wrote on September 15. This reflected the men's eagerness to reach St. Louis. At times the boats had to maneuver cautiously among half-sunken or floating trees. The men spent as little time as possible hunting and ate the wild plums that were abundant near the river. They called the plums pawpaws. On this day there was no meat, and Clark wrote, "the party appear perfectly contented and tell us that they can live very well on the pappaws."

❧ September 20, 1806

Shortly after noon, the men spotted some cows on the riverbank—evidence that they had reached settlers. This "Caused a Shout to be raised for joy." Farther downstream the boats landed at a village called Charrette, where the explorers were fed "a very agreeable supper." People in the village and in trading boats anchored there were astonished that the explorers were still alive.

❧ September 22, 1806

It rained heavily this morning, yet the explorers were dry inside the houses of the people of St. Charles, the community the men had visited on May 21,1804. They appreciated the hospitality, though the odd feeling of being in a comfortable bed probably caused some to sleep poorly.

❧ September 23–25, 1806

About noon on September 23, the Corps of Discovery had reached St. Louis, completing its extraordinary eight-thousand-mile journey. The captains allowed the men to fire their rifles as a salute. As the boats neared shore, the air was filled with the sounds of men laughing and shouting—and of a large black dog barking. In his journal Sergeant John Ordway wrote, "the people gathred on the Shore and Huzzared three cheers."

A whirlwind of dinners and other celebrations followed. This evening the explorers were guests at a dinner and ball.

Glasses were raised in many toasts, the final one to "Captains Lewis and Clark—Their perilous services endear them to every American heart."

When Meriwether Lewis walked the streets of St. Louis, many people stopped him to ask questions or simply to shake the hand of a great explorer and hero. And some of them probably reached down to touch another American hero, the dog at his side.

Afterword

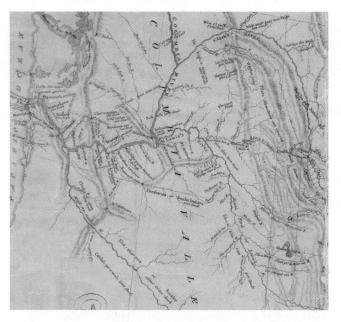

This is the western portion of William Clark's historic map, which is more than four feet wide. He completed it at Fort Clatsop on February 14, 1806.

For nearly two and a half years the members of the Corps of Discovery were joined in a grand adventure considered the greatest expedition in U.S. history. Then it ended, and the explorers went on with their lives.

Few details are known about the later lives of most of the men who served in the expedition as U.S. Army privates. Some remained in the army and fought in the War of 1812. Nearly every man on the expedition received money and 320 acres of land as payment for his services, so some became farmers.

Some married, had children, and led long lives, but many died young because so little was known about treating diseases in the early 1800s. Joseph Field died within a year of the expedition's end. His brother Reubin married and settled in Kentucky.

When Patrick Gass died in 1870 at the age of ninety-nine, he was the last known survivor of the expedition. As a sergeant he had kept a journal, and his brief account of the expedition was the first published, in 1807.

John Colter, who stayed in the West rather than return to St. Louis, spent several years trapping animals for fur and exploring the Rocky Mountains. For a time, people made fun of his reports of a spectacular area with hot springs and geysers that spewed water high into the air. Today that place is part of Yellowstone National Park. In 1808 Colter narrowly escaped from an attack by Blackfeet Indians. He married and settled down in Missouri but was dead by 1813.

George Drouillard helped establish a trading post near the Three Forks of the Missouri River. However, both he and John Potts, an army private on the expedition, were killed by Blackfeet no later than 1810. Private George Shannon was wounded by Arikara Indians in 1807 during an attempt to return the chief Big White to his people. Shannon had a leg amputated but lived to help prepare a history of the Lewis and Clark expedition and to be elected a U.S. senator from Missouri.

Toussaint Charbonneau found work along the Missouri River, mostly as an interpreter for the U.S. government. He lived to be about eighty. Little is known about his wife, Sacagawea. She had a second child, a daughter named Lizette. In 1809 Sacagawea and Charbonneau brought their son, Pomp, to St. Louis and turned him over to William Clark's guardianship. Eventually Lizette was also placed in Clark's care.

As for Sacagawea herself, while some claim that she lived a long life, most historians believe that she died in 1812, while still a young woman. To most people of those times Sacagawea was a person of little importance. As time passed and more was learned about the Lewis and Clark expedition, her unique role was recognized. In the year 2000 the U.S. government issued a gold-colored one-dollar coin in her honor. It became enormously popular. Its engraving shows Sacagawea with Pomp on her back.

The Sacagawea dollar coin.

Pomp, or Jean Baptiste Charbonneau, went to school in St. Louis. He lived in Europe for six years. After returning to the United States he worked as a guide and interpreter for western explorers, sometimes living with the Hidatsa. He died in Oregon at age sixty-one.

William Clark's slave, York, is mentioned numerous times in the journals. He helped haul boats upstream, carried heavy loads, hunted bison, and in general did the same work as the other men. Because he was a slave, however, he did not receive the money or land that

At various places in his journal Clark used Sacagawea's name, but he also called her Charbonneau's wife, Janey, or simply the Squaw. On July 6 he wrote, "The Squar pointed to the gap through which she said we must pass." Although Sacagawea was helpful as a guide through unfamiliar country on the return trip, and somewhat on the way West, Old Toby of the Shoshone gave the most crucial help in guiding the expedition westward through the Rockies. Sacagawea's greatest contribution was as an interpreter with the Shoshone, and simply as a woman whose presence signified that the expedition was not a war party.

the others had been awarded as payment. Not until about 1811, five years after the expedition returned, did Clark free York, giving him horses and a wagon to help him get started in the business of transporting freight. Sometime before 1832 York died of cholera in Tennessee.

Not long after the expedition returned, William Clark married a young woman he had long known—his cousin Julia Hancock. (In fact, he had named a river that flowed into the Upper Missouri after her.) They named their first-born son Meriwether Lewis Clark. They eventually had four more children. After Julia died, Clark married a widow, adopted her three children, and fathered two more sons and perhaps a daughter.

Clark's map of the western two-thirds of the continent was of great value for several decades after the expedition. He had a successful career as governor of the Missouri Territory and as Superintendent of Indian Affairs. He died in 1838 in St. Louis at the age of sixty-nine.

In these days of quick reports from news media, it may be difficult to imagine life on the frontier in 1806. There was no newspaper in the little town of St. Louis; the nearest newspaper was in Kentucky. Furthermore, most news published was in the form of letters, which is why Lewis wrote a letter about the expedition to his parents and Clark's parents. News of the expedition's return was not published in Pittsburgh until October 28 or in Washington until November 3, 1806.

As for Meriwether Lewis, within an hour or two of reaching St. Louis he began writing a report to be mailed to President Jefferson. Then he wrote a letter from himself and Clark, giving some details about the expedition that would appear in newspapers. In the weeks following the expedition's triumphant return to St. Louis, both Clark and Lewis were honored at many dinners. Not until the end of 1806 did Lewis meet with Jefferson in Washington. They spread Clark's map of the West on the floor and examined it on hands and knees. Lewis spent the winter with the president, telling him all about the expedition.

Meriwether Lewis had accomplished everything that the president had asked. He had found a good route to the Pacific. It was not his fault that North American geography offered no easy water passage. Nor was it his fault that his efforts to encourage peaceful relations among Indian tribes were not successful.

The basic news of the expedition's success encouraged trappers, traders, and explorers to head westward. The journals that Lewis and Clark kept were rich with much more information about the lands and waters of the West and about plants, animals, and native peoples. However, the information was of little value if it was not made public. It was Lewis's job to have a full report of the expedition published, and Jefferson urged him to do so as soon as possible.

The president, however, also rewarded Lewis by appointing him governor of the Louisiana Territory, headquartered in St. Louis. The job was difficult, and Lewis was not well suited for it. Once hailed as a hero, Lewis was criticized as an ineffective governor. His troubles grew. Women he courted were not interested in marrying him—perhaps because he had become a heavy drinker. He lost money in land speculation and fell into debt. Month after month passed, and Lewis made little progress in editing the journals for publication. He was failing at this hugely important task.

Lewis's life, so full of confidence and hope in 1806, by

1809 had turned to one of failure and despair. In September of that year he set out overland for Washington. Along the way he wrote a will. He was drinking heavily and acting strangely, sometimes talking violently to himself. On October 10, 1809, Meriwether Lewis took a room in an inn along a Tennessee road called the Natchez Trace. In the early hours of October 11 he shot himself to death. He was thirty-five years old.

Some historians claim that Lewis was murdered, but the evidence points strongly to suicide. Both Jefferson and Clark were sad about Lewis's death, but both knew him well and accepted the idea that he might take his own life. His death further delayed publication of the expedition's journals. A short version appeared in 1814. Not until 1904 were the complete journals, in eight volumes, finally published. As a result of this delay, Lewis and Clark were not credited with the discovery of many animals and plants that they were the first to describe.

For nearly two centuries people have wondered what had happened to Lewis's dog. Seaman is not mentioned in the journals after July 15, 1806. Clark's journal ends two days after the expedition's September 23, 1806, arrival in St. Louis. Since the dog's name does not appear during an earlier eight-month period, not mentioning Seaman for about two months would not be remarkable. However, on July 16, Lewis and three men set out on horseback to explore the Marias River. Did he take his dog along? If so, Seaman would have fallen far behind as Lewis and his men fled from the Blackfeet, racing their horses a hundred miles in less than a day. Even if Seaman had been able to reach the Missouri, the boats would have already carried his master and the other explorers far downstream. Seaman would have been abandoned—left alone to face grizzly bears and other dangers in the wilderness.

Some historians believe that Lewis probably did not take Seaman overland to explore the Marias River. Instead he probably left him to guard the men working above the Great Falls on the Missouri, where grizzly bears were so abundant. Also, Lewis knew his group would be riding horseback on hot July days, and had learned that his dog suffered greatly from heat and cactus thorns when traveling overland. According to this theory, Seaman would have been aboard a canoe or the pirogue, greeting Lewis when he returned to the Missouri.

What happened to Seaman? For nearly two centuries historians researched old letters, newspapers, and other documents to solve this mystery. Finally, in February 2000, historian James Holmberg reported some important clues.

Records from 1812 show that William Clark gave some items—"Curiosities"—to a small museum in Alexandria, Virginia. A fire in 1871 destroyed much of the museum's collection, including presumably whatever objects Clark had donated. However, long before the fire an educator named Timothy Alden visited the museum and wrote about an unusual object displayed there.

Alden was a well-respected historian. He collected epitaphs and inscriptions from monuments, cemetery headstones, and other sources. In his 1814 book, *A Collection of American Epitaphs and Inscriptions with Occasional Notes,* entry 916 is an inscription he found on a dog collar in a museum in Alexandria, Virginia:

"The greatest traveller of my species. My name is SEAMAN, the dog of captain Meriwether Lewis, whom I accompanied to the Pacifick ocean through the interior of the continent of North America."

Timothy Alden then wrote these words about the inscription:

The foregoing was copied from the collar, in the Alexandria museum, which the late gov. Lewis's dog wore after his return from the western coast of America. The fidelity and attachment of this animal were remarkable. After the melancholy exit of gov. Lewis, his dog would not depart for a moment from his lifeless remains; and when they were deposited in the earth no gentle means could draw him from the spot of interment. He refused to take every kind of food, which was offered him, and actually pined away and died with grief upon his master's grave!*

*The collar inscription and Alden's words about it are quoted from "Seaman's Fate?" by James Holmberg, in the February 2000 issue of *We Proceeded On*, the journal of the Lewis and Clark Trail Heritage Foundation.

Actual Entries About Seaman in the
Journals of the
Lewis and Clark Expedition

September 11, 1803—Lewis reports his dog caught squirrels.

September 15, 1803—Lewis reports Seaman catching more squirrels.

November 16, 1803—Lewis tells of offer of beaver skins in trade for his dog.

July 4, 1804—Clark includes Seaman in list of explorers.

July 5, 1804—Clark tells of Seaman driving beaver from their lodge.

July 14, 1804—Ordway reports that Seaman swam after elk.

August 25, 1804—Clark tells of Seaman overheating on hike.

April 18, 1805—Ordway writes that Seaman "b. out" (brought out?) a dead goose from water.

April 22, 1805—Lewis suspects that bison calf frightened by Seaman.

April 25, 1805—Lewis and Clark report that Seaman returned after being absent all night.

April 26, 1805—Ordway writes that Seaman caught a swimming pronghorn.

April 29, 1805—Lewis refers to Seaman catching a pronghorn, probably that of April 26.

May 5, 1805—Both Lewis and Clark write about Seaman catching another pronghorn.

May 19, 1805—Lewis, Clark, and Ordway all write about Seaman being bitten by a beaver.

May 29, 1805—Lewis, Clark, and Ordway all tell how Seaman caused bison bull to change direction as it ran through camp.

June 19, 1805—Lewis reports Seaman barking at bison near camp.

June 27, 1805—Lewis tells of Seaman barking at grizzly bears near camp.

June 28, 1805—Lewis praises Seaman again as guard against bears.

July 15, 1805—Lewis tells of Seaman catching a deer in the river.

July 21, 1805—Lewis mentions Seaman catching geese.

July 26, 1805—Lewis writes that his dog suffers from the barbed seeds of needlegrass.

August 17, 1805—Both Lewis and Clark mention that the Shoshone admire Seaman.

April 11, 1806—Both Lewis and Clark write about Indian attempt to steal Seaman.

May 8, 1806—Lewis, Clark, and Ordway report that Seaman caught a wounded deer.

May 23, 1806—Both Lewis and Clark write that Seaman caught another wounded deer.

July 5, 1806—Both Lewis and Clark write that a creek was named in honor of the expedition's dog.

July 7, 1806—Lewis reports that Seaman was "much worried" about a wounded moose.

July 15, 1806—Lewis tells of his dog howling in torment from mosquitoes—the last mention of Seaman in the journals.

Bibliography and Further Reading

Main Sources

The most important source of day-to-day activities and quotations was the University of Nebraska Press edition of the expedition's journals and maps, edited by Gary Moulton. These volumes can be found in some public libraries and in libraries of many colleges and universities.

Anderson, Irving. "Sacajawea? Sakakawea? Sacagawea? Spelling-
   Pronounciation-Meaning." *We Proceeded On.* (Summer 1975): 10–12.
Holmberg, James. "Seaman's Fate?" *We Proceeded On.* (February 2000): 7–9.
Jackson, Donald. "Call Him a Good Old Dog, But Don't Call Him Scannon."
   We Proceeded On. (August 1985): 5–8.
Moulton, Gary, ed. *The Journals of the Lewis and Clark Expedition.* 13 vols.
   Lincoln: University of Nebraska Press, 1983–2001.
Plamondon, Martin II. "Decision at Chinook Point." *We Proceeded On.*
   (May 2001): 13–19.
Ronda, James. *Lewis and Clark Among the Indians.* Lincoln: University of
   Nebraska Press, 1984.

Secondary Sources

Ambrose, Stephen. *Lewis & Clark: Voyage of Discovery.* Washington, D.C.:
   National Geographic Society, 1998.
Ambrose, Stephen. *Undaunted Courage: Meriwether Lewis, Thomas Jefferson,
   and the Opening of the American West.* New York: Simon and Shuster,
1996.
Duncan, Dayton, and Ken Burns. *Lewis and Clark: The Journey of the Corps
of*
   Discovery. New York: Alfred Knopf, 1997.
Fisher, Ron. "Lewis and Clark, Naturalist-Explorers." *National Geographic.*
   (October 1998): 77–93.
Lavender, David. *The Way to the Western Sea.* New York: Harper and Row,
1988.
Ronda, James. *Finding the West: Explorations with Lewis and Clark.*
   Albuquerque: University of New Mexico Press, 2001.
Schmidt, Thomas, and Jeremy Schmidt. *The Saga of Lewis and Clark: Into the
   Uncharted West.* New York: DK Publishing, 1999.

Recommended Children's Books

Blumberg, Rhoda. *The Incredible Journey of Lewis and Clark.* New York: Lothrop, Lee and Shepard, 1987.

Edwards, Judith. *Lewis and Clark's Journey of Discovery.* Springfield, N.J.: Enslow Publishers, 1999.

Fitz-Gerald, Christine. *The World's Great Explorers: Meriwether Lewis and William Clark.* Chicago: Children's Press, 1991.

Herbert, Janis. *Lewis and Clark for Kids.* Chicago: Chicago Review Press, 2000.

Karwoski, Gail. *Seaman: The Dog Who Explored the West with Lewis and Clark.* Atlanta: Peachtree Publishers, 1999.

Morley, Jacqueline. *Expedition Across America: The Story of Lewis and Clark.* New York: Franklin Watts, 1998.

Patent, Dorothy Hinshaw. *Animals on the Trail with Lewis and Clark.* New York: Clarion, 2002.

St. George, Judith. *Sacagawea.* New York: Putnam, 1997.

Santella, Andrew. *Lewis and Clark.* New York: Franklin Watts, 2001.

Schanzer, Rosalyn. *How We Crossed the West: The Adventures of Lewis and Clark.* Washington, D.C.: National Geographic, 1997.

For More Information

The Lewis and Clark Trail Heritage Foundation publishes the historical journal *We Proceeded On,* maps, and other publications about the expedition. More than thirty chapters of this organization are active across the nation. Contact the Foundation at P.O. Box 3434, Great Falls, MT 59403; phone: 1-888-701-3434; Web: www.lewisandclark.org.

The National Council of the Lewis and Clark Bicentennial is the best single source of information about bicentennial activities planned by federal, state, and tribal governments. Address mail to the council at Lewis & Clark College, 0615 SW Palatine Hill Road, Portland, OR 97219; phone: 1-888-999-1803; Web: www.http://lewisandclark200.org.

The "Lewis and Clark National Historic Trail" is a map of the expedition's route, with the location of more than eighty parks, viewing sites, and exhibits shown and described. The free map is available from the National Park Service, Office of Public Affairs, 1849 C Street, N.W., Washington, D.C. 20240, or from the Lewis and Clark National Historic Trail, 1709 Jackson Street, Omaha, Nebraska 68102.

Index

145

148

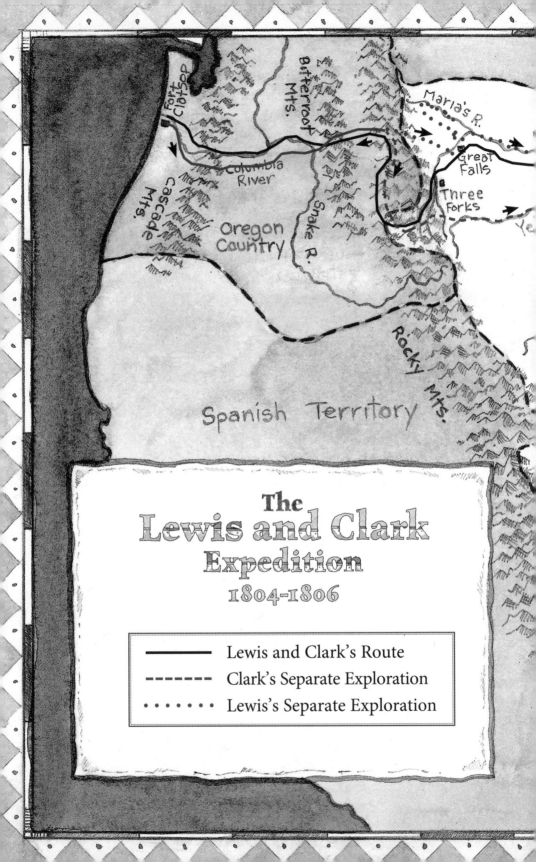

British North America

ri R.

ne R.

Fort
Mandan

Mississippi R.

Louisiana
Purchase

Indiana
Territory

Ohio

Ohio R.

Kentucky

Tennessee

Mississippi
Territory

W. Florida

N

100   200 MI

0 200KM

GULF
OF
MEXICO